STONE'S BRIGADE
AND THE
FIGHT FOR THE
McPHERSON FARM

Col. Roy Stone
149th Regt., Pa. Vol. Inf.
(USAMHI, from an engraving)

Col. Langhorne Wister
150th Regt., Pa. Vol. Inf.
(USAMHI)

Col. Edmund L. Dana
143rd Regt., Pa. Vol. Inf.
(USAMHI)

STONE'S BRIGADE
AND THE
FIGHT FOR THE
McPHERSON FARM

BATTLE OF GETTYSBURG
July 1, 1863

James J. Dougherty

PUBLISHER'S NOTE

The headquarters of Combined Publishing are located midway between Valley Forge and the Germantown battlefield, on the outskirts of Philadelphia. From its beginnings, our company has been steeped in the oldest traditions of American history and publishing. Our historic surroundings help maintain our focus on history and our books strive to uphold the standards of style, quality and durability first established by the earliest bookmakers of Germantown and Philadelphia so many years ago. Our famous monk-and-console logo reflects our commitment to the modern and yet historic enterprise of publishing.

We call ourselves Combined Publishing because we have always felt that our goals could only be achieved through a "combined" effort by authors, publishers and readers. We have always tried to maintain maximum communication between these three key players in the reading experience.

We are always interested in hearing from prospective authors about new books in our field. We also like to hear from our readers and invite you to contact us at our offices in Pennsylvania with any questions, comments or suggestions, or if you have difficulty finding our books at a local bookseller.

For information, address:
Combined Publishing
P.O. Box 307
Conshohocken, PA 19428
E-mail: combined@combinedpublishing.com
Web: www.combinedpublishing.com
Orders: 1-800-418-6065

Cataloging in Publication data available from the Library of Congress

ISBN 1-58097-032-X

Printed in the United States of America.

Dedication

Dedicated to the memory of my father, James William Dougherty, a proud Irishman from the Clann O'Dochartaigh who taught me as a child to revere the Gettysburg battlefield and the epic struggle that occurred there in the summer of 1863. Sadly, he was taken before his time.

"If we do meet again, why we shall smile; If not, why then this parting was well made."

—William Shakespeare

Acknowledgements

I would like to gratefully acknowledge the invaluable assistance offered by the many friends and historians who aided me in this endeavor, principal among them John Heiser of the Gettysburg National Military Park, who endured my many visits to the library and answered innumerable tedious questions; Bruce Craig, also of the Gettysburg National Military Park, who graciously assisted me in searching for an obscure file in their closed archives on the restoration of the McPherson barn; Tim Smith, Licensed Battlefield Guide, who provided assistance on Stone's route of march and on the many nuances of the John Burns story; Steve Zerbe, private Research Archivist, who led me to many useful sources; and the staffs of the Civil War Library and Museum in Philadelphia, the Adams County Historical Society, the Wyoming Historical and Geological Society, and the United States Army Military History Institute in Carlisle. I would be derelict in my duties if I neglected to mention my dear friend Vince Gasbarro, an accomplished Gettysburg scholar, who read the manuscript and offered a number of valuable suggestions for its improvement and who toured the field with me on various occasions in an effort to interpret its topography. Above all, my everlasting love and gratitude to my best friend and faithful wife Anne and my daughter Dana for their unwavering support and encouragement throughout the process of writing this book. I'm thrilled to know that they too share a great love of Gettysburg.

Contents

Preface   9

1. Organization of the "Bucktail Brigade"   11
2. Spring 1863   21
3. The Manor of Maske   27
4. Stone Takes Position on the McPherson Farm   33
5. Daniel's North Carolinians Attack   51
6. Collapse of the Second Brigade   71
7. Retreat Through the Town   99
8. July 2, 1863   107
9. July 3, 1863   113
10. Stone's Casualties on the McPherson Farm   119
11. Post-battle History of the McPherson Farm   135

Epilogue   147

Appendixes

The Court-martial of Brigadier General Thomas A. Rowley   151
The Story of John L. Burns   155
Succession of Brigade Command, July 1, 1863   161
Bibliography   166
Index   175

Maps

Stone's March to Gettysburg 24

Stone Takes Position on the McPherson Farm, 11:45 A.M. 40

The 149th Pennsylvania Takes Position on the
Chambersburg Pike, 12:30 P.M. 46

The 143rd Pennsylvania Takes Position on the
Chambersburg Pike, 1:00 P.M. 48

Iverson and Daniel Attack, 1:30 P.M. 52

Daniel's Initial Attack Is Repulsed, 1:45–2:00 P.M. 54

The 149th Pennsylvania Occupies the Railroad Cut,
2:00–2:15 P.M. 56

Daniel Sweeps the 149th Pennsylvania from the Cut,
2:15–2:30 P.M. 60

Right Wing of the 150th Pennsylvania Takes Position on
the Chambersburg Pike, 2:30–2:45 P.M. 64

The 149th and 150th Pennsylvania Retake the Cut,
2:45–3:00 P.M. 66

Daniel Crosses the Cut; Brockenbrough Attacks;
The Iron Brigade Retires, 3:00 P.M. 72

Stone's Position Collapses: Fight for the Colors of the
149th Pennsylvania, 3:30 P.M. 76

Last Stand on Seminary Ridge, 4:00 P.M. 94

Cemetery Hill, Night of July 1, 1863 104

July 3, 1863 114

The McPherson Farm 138

Preface

"We have come to stay!"

The battle of Gettysburg, fought over the first three days of July 1863, was the greatest epic ever contested in the Western Hemisphere. It has been well documented in the diaries, letters, and newspaper articles of the men who fought there. Later it was interpreted by historians in books, magazines, and most recently, on the Internet. The actions of regiments, brigades, divisions, and corps have been exhaustively studied, frequently on a microscopic level. Unfortunately, the heroic struggle for the McPherson Farm that raged in the late morning and early afternoon of July 1, 1863, is largely forgotten in light of the more popular accounts of the fighting that involved Buford's cavalry, the Iron Brigade, and Cutler's fight for the Railroad Cut. Some historians have even gone so far as to call the time that Stone's brigade took possession of the farm as a *"lull"* in the battle. In light of this study, we can now say that this is a highly inaccurate description. It is true that the fierce action of the morning had briefly waned. However, during this "lull," Stone's brigade was subjected to a prolonged artillery barrage and the costly harassment of Rebel skirmishers, both of which resulted in the wounding and death of a number of Bucktails. Perhaps from the safety of Seminary Ridge there appeared to be a period of calm on the field. But from the perspective of Stone's troops, the term "lull" would have been considered a rather relative term.

Aside from being misrepresented, there are a number of popular accounts of the battle that fail to mention the gallant struggle that occurred on and around Edward McPherson's property. Those that do, merely describe the presence of Stone's brigade almost as an afterthought. With few exceptions, the versions that do attempt to describe the fighting there are often misinterpreted, adding more confusion to an already complicated and misunderstood portion of the battle. In any case, justice has not been done to the men, Union and Confederate, who fought and died on this portion of the field. This account of the action involving Stone's brigade on July 1 is intended to be accurate and objective, relying as much as possible on the primary source information of those who fought there or may have witnessed the action. For the first time this represents a comprehensive explanation of the fighting involving all three of Stone's regiments.

Though originally begun as a study of the role the 143rd Pennsylvania played during the First Day, I found that concentrating on a single regiment of Stone's brigade would result in further injustice. In addition, I found that because the three regiments of Stone's brigade fought in such close proximity, the commands often mixing together, it was impossible to tell an accurate story of one without describing the movements and actions of the others.

As may be expected, firsthand accounts of the fighting are frequently in conflict. What one man may have seen on the left of his regiment may have gone completely unnoticed to those in the center or right. Often times, soldiers were so focused on what was happening in their immediate front that they were frequently and understandably unaware of what was happening around them. For this reason, their accounts must be taken in context. Individually they tell a myopic story, but taken as a whole, these accounts give an accurate, colorful, and often humorous chronicle of the day's events.

Because of the complex nature of the fighting that occurred in the vicinity of the farm and owing to the competitive character of Stone's regiments, a number of controversies surrounding the day's action surfaced after the war. I have attempted to examine as many relevant primary sources as was necessary to clarify some of these issues. The result is an account of the fight for the McPherson Farm that I think Stone's veterans would feel finally does justice to their many sacrifices. Having fought and died defending their home state, they deserve no less.

Chapter 1

ORGANIZATION OF THE "BUCKTAIL BRIGADE"

"...honor on the old Commonwealth."

IN LATE APRIL 1861, a few weeks after the attack on Fort Sumter, 26-year-old businessman Roy Stone left Warren County, Pennsylvania, on his way to Pittsburgh. He was accompanied by one hundred or so lumbermen whom he had recruited to join one of the new three-month regiments. But when they reached Pittsburgh, the men were turned away because the state's troop quota had already been filled. While awaiting their fate, they were notified that they would be accepted as a company in Thomas Kane's new regiment assembling in Harrisburg.[1]

The regiments that exceeded the number authorized by the Federal government were designated "reserves." Thomas Kane's new regiment went by various official and unofficial titles: Kane's Rifles, the First Pennsylvania Rifle Reserves, the 42nd Regiment, the 13th Pennsylvania Reserves, and eventually, the "Bucktails." In May 1862, a full year after they organized, the 42nd Pennsylvania was divided into two battalions. The first battalion, four companies under Lieutenant Colonel Thomas Kane, was sent to the Shenandoah, and the second, six companies under Major Roy Stone, was assigned to the Pennsylvania Reserves of the Army of the Potomac, then operating on the Peninsula in Virginia.[2]

1. Richard E. Matthews, The *149th Pennsylvania Volunteer Infantry Unit in the Civil War,* (Jefferson, 1994), 1.
2. Ibid., 2.

In July 1862, Special Orders No. 196 arrived from Major General George B. McClellan ordering Stone to return promptly to Pennsylvania and to report to the Superintendent of the Recruiting Service. Having won a reputation for "brilliant achievements" on the field of battle, Stone had been chosen to return to his home state to organize a new brigade of Pennsylvania "Bucktails." The original Bucktails (42nd Pennsylvania) had become known as skilled marksmen and skirmishers while serving under Stone on the Peninsula in 1862. "So marked was their bravery, that they had become the pride of their own soldiers, and the terror of the foe," penned one patriotic historian.[3] Colonel Hugh McNeil, the original commander of the Bucktails, deemed the New York-born and Pennsylvania-raised Stone as "eminently qualified" for command of the new brigade. McNeil, who was later killed at Antietam, said, "A Bucktail Brigade of light infantry would reflect additional honor on the old Commonwealth."[4] This met with instant favor from Pennsylvania Governor Andrew Curtin who recognized that a second Bucktail command would bring further notoriety to his state.

The original Bucktails received their name because of the deer tails worn on their caps, supposedly symbolizing their marksmanship. According to William H. Rauch, the Bucktail's regimental historian, a soldier by the name of James Landregan from McKean County had noticed a deer's hide hanging outside a butcher shop in Smethport, Pennsylvania. "Crossing the street, he pulled out his penknife, cut off the deer's tail and stuck it in his cap." Colonel Thomas L. Kane seized upon the idea and commanded that from then on the regiment would be known as the "Bucktails." Soon deer tails were on the caps of all the new recruits.[5]

The original Bucktails were outraged upon learning that the governor had decided to raise a new brigade of Pennsylvanians and to confer the Bucktail name on them. They claimed that they alone were entitled to the Bucktail name, having rightfully earned it, and nicknamed the new regiments the "Bogus Bucktails." But the idea for the new Bucktail command had come from Colonel McNeil him-

3. Samuel P. Bates, *History of the Pennsylvania Volunteers, 1861-1865*, 5 vols. (Harrisburg, Pennsylvania: State Printer, 1869-71), 5: 611.
4. Ibid.
5. William H. Rauch, *History of the Bucktails*. (Philadelphia, Pennsylvania, 1906), 11.

self. The Bucktail name may have been misappropriated for the prideful purpose of filling the ranks of the new companies, but its desired effect was achieved. The motivation of the new regiments as a result of their title was clearly evident. Though the debate raged throughout the war and for years afterward, both the original Bucktails and the "Bogus Bucktails" of Stone's brigade served nobly and could be proud of their honorable accomplishments.

The One Hundred Forty-Ninth Regiment
Pennsylvania Volunteers

While the debate continued, August advertisements in Pennsylvania newspapers requested men to fill the ranks of four new Bucktail regiments. This resulted in the raising of 20 companies of men in only 20 days. Indeed, this was an opportunity for able young Pennsylvanians to enlist in a proud regiment with experienced leaders while serving alongside their family and friends. While patriotism and pride may have played a role in inspiring enlistees, the promised bounty, no doubt, also contributed to their decision as well. Lumbermen, farmers, and miners from Potter, Tioga, Lycoming, Clearfield, Clarion, Lebanon, Allegheny, Luzerne, Mifflin, and Huntingdon counties hastened to join.[6]

Harrisburg's Camp Curtin played host to the new recruits for their initial organization. Camp Curtin was given the task of organizing the masses of men into specific commands. Once assigned, outfitted, and armed, they would be forwarded elsewhere for training. The camp was built on the county fairgrounds with a pavilion and racetrack in the center. Before long, thousands of new recruits began to alter the camp. Poor sanitation caused foul smells, disease, and swarms of flies. Enforcement of sanitation rules on the new recruits was difficult, since these recruits were in camp only temporarily.[7]

Many of the young men who had arrived at Camp Curtin had never received any formal discipline. It would take time before their

6. Samuel P. Bates, *History of the Pennsylvania Volunteers*, 4: 612.
7. Richard Matthews, *The 149th Pennsylvania*, 19-20.

commanders would earn the type of respect that evolved into the military discipline required to manage troops in the field. But the social atmosphere that thrived in the camp helped to bring the men together into a cohesive organization. Pride developed over the two weeks that the men stayed in camp and it was this pride that company commanders eventually developed into military discipline.

During the last week of August 1861, ten companies were officially organized into the 149th Regiment Pennsylvania Volunteer Infantry and their uniforms, accoutrements, and prized Enfield rifles were issued. Some also received their much-anticipated $50 bounty. On August 30, with Confederate troops threatening Washington, D.C., Colonel Roy Stone's 149th Pennsylvania was herded into railcars and rushed to the Washington defenses. Though he had originally planned to raise four Bucktail regiments, the crisis outside the capital forced his departure with only one.[8]

September found the green troops assigned to various details throughout the capital. Some were assigned guard duty while others performed miscellaneous labor. This was surely demoralizing for men who had enlisted to be part of an elite regiment with a name symbolizing a reputation for hard fighting. By mid-month however, hoping to improve the spirits of the men, Colonel Stone brought the companies together for the purpose of strenuous training. Stone was keenly aware that they would soon see combat and he intended to make sure the boys were ready. Fifteen- or sixteen-hour days were not uncommon and intense drilling soon transformed the troops into a proud fighting force. Before long however, the troops were assigned more fatigue duty around the city and the tedium resumed.[9]

By October and November, exposure to the diseases rampant in Washington hospitalized many. The troops remained hopeful that their day would eventually come with assignment to a fighting brigade. But first they would have to endure a long, hard winter in Washington.[10]

---

8. Ibid., 21.
9. Ibid., 31.
10. Ibid., 35. Consult this source for a detailed description of camp life while in Washington.

The One Hundred Fiftieth Regiment
Pennsylvania Volunteers

In August 1862, while Colonel Stone was organizing the 149th Pennsylvania, Captain Langhorne Wister, a Philadelphia native and veteran commander of Company B, 42nd Pennsylvania, was recruiting four new companies of Bucktails in the City of Brotherly Love. Wister had been wounded in the ankle at Gaines's Mill and had requested permission to return to Philadelphia to assist in the recruitment of the new Bucktail brigade. His efforts quickly resulted in the raising of four companies. The first two, Companies A and B, were recruited entirely in Germantown, while Companies E and F came from Phoenixville and sections of Philadelphia. From the regimental recruiting office on the north side of Chestnut Street, between Fifth and Sixth Streets, Adjutant Richard L. Ashurst designed recruiting posters advertising a $25 bounty for enlistment plus one month's pay up front and $75 at the end of the war. This, along with the proud Bucktail name, provided a valuable incentive much as it had to the men of the 149th Pennsylvania.[11]

Despite the rapid filling of the ranks in Companies A and B, Companies E and F were slow to grow. In an effort to obtain more men, Wister hired a flatbed furniture car which was decorated with the national colors and placards reading, "Enlist in the Bucktail Brigade!" From poles attached to the vehicle hung a vast array of bucktails that were given to expected recruits. The car was then drawn through the city by horse followed by fife and drums to draw attention. Their efforts were successful and by nightfall they had drawn in enough men to fill out the remaining companies.[12]

During the last week of August, Colonel Wister's four companies were camped in the Nicetown section of the city opposite Logan's Run with the 114th Pennsylvania (Collis's Zouaves), who were themselves awaiting orders to march.[13]

On September 1 and 2, 1862, Companies A, B, E, and F boarded trains in West Philadelphia and set out for Harrisburg's Camp

---

11. Thomas Chamberlin, *History of the One Hundred and Fiftieth Regiment Pennsylvania Volunteers.* (Philadelphia, 1905), 20-21.
12. Ibid., 22-23.
13. Ibid., 23.

Curtin. The five additional companies that would fill out the command arrived at Camp Curtin at the same time. Companies C, H, I, and K were recruited in Crawford County with the assistance of Captain Henry S. Huidekoper. Captain Henry W. Crotzer had recruited Company D in Union County and Captain Horatio Bell had assembled Company G in McKean County. The command now numbered 928 officers and men.[14]

Originally designated the 143rd Regiment Pennsylvania Volunteers, their designation was changed when the regiment's lieutenant colonel, a Crawford County boy who had recently studied tactics and squad drill at the elite Harvard University, was given a choice of identifications. Henry S. Huidekoper was given a choice of designations between 145 and 155[15] by Adjutant General A. L. Russell. He chose the number "150" because it was a "good round number."[16]

During the first few days of September, Huidekoper led the regiment to the arsenal in Harrisburg where they were armed with the Enfield rifle. Despite protests about the rifle's weight and what they considered its "limited range," with practice these rifles would become a deadly tool in the hands of these skilled Pennsylvania hunters. It would take another six weeks to receive a standard bearing their regimental designation.[17]

On Friday morning, September 5, 1862, the 150th Pennsylvania boarded trains for Washington, D.C. Upon arrival, and following some brief training, Companies D and K were assigned to duties at the Soldiers' Home, the summer residence of President Abraham Lincoln. Company A was detailed to the Soldiers' Rest near Baltimore Depot (Company D would later join them), and Company K was later assigned the duty of President Lincoln's escort, where they would remain until after his assassination.[18]

For the rest of the regiment, the fall and winter of 1862 was filled with the tedium of training and various guard duties at the many hospitals in and about Washington, D.C. The officers on the other hand, "were by no means overburdened with work, and found abundant time—particularly in the evenings—for social

---

14. Ibid., 29.
15. John F. Krumweide, "A July Afternoon on McPherson's Ridge," *Gettysburg Magazine*, 21: 26.
16. Thomas Chamberlin, *History of the One Hundred and Fiftieth Regiment*, 30.
17. Ibid., 30.
18. Ibid., 38. George Ashmun, "Union Light Guards," *Magazine of History*, 3, No. 4 (April, 1906). Copy Ford's Theatre National Historic Site.

enjoyment." It seems that a number of the officers—Colonel Wister, Lieutenant Colonel Huidekoper, and Adjutant Ashurst among them—"having no mandate for special duty and finding themselves without occupation," decided to make themselves as comfortable as possible and rented a furnished apartment near the intersection of Twelfth and M Streets. With the arrival of Mrs. Ashurst, who tended to the housekeeping, the residence soon became the "social center" of the regiment.[19]

On October 21, the 149th and 150th Pennsylvania were drawn up in line and received their much anticipated state colors. Following the presentation made by Secretary Thomas, on Governor Curtin's behalf, Colonels Stone and Wister made some brief remarks and led the men in three cheers for the governor.[20]

On November 11, the 143rd Pennsylvania arrived from Camp Curtin. Previous contact with the officers of that regiment had resulted in a "hearty co-operation" between the commands and Colonels Stone and Wister had made a special effort to see that the 143rd was brigaded with their Bucktails. In the months to follow, their efforts would be rewarded.[21]

On February 14, 1863, the various details of the 150th Pennsylvania, except Company K which stayed behind with the president, were relieved of their duties and ordered to pack up camp "so as to be ready at a moment's notice." That notice came on the morning of the 15th when the 149th and 150th Pennsylvania were gathered together and loaded onboard the steamship *Louisiana*. At long last, they had been assigned to the Army of the Potomac and on February 16 learned that they were to be designated the Second Brigade, Third Division, First Corps.[22]

The One Hundred Forty-Third Regiment Pennsylvania Volunteers

Edmund L. Dana was educated as an engineer but was practicing law when war came in 1861. Having found an aptitude for fight-

---

19. Thomas Chamberlin, *History of the One Hundred and Fiftieth Regiment*, 47-51.
20. Ibid., 46.
21. Ibid., 49.
22. Ibid., 60-61.

ing during the Mexican War, he was the obvious choice for command of the 143rd Pennsylvania when it was organized in the summer and fall of 1862. During that period, Dana was instrumental in recruiting, organizing, and training the newly formed regiment. Owing to his experience and education, he was commissioned colonel on October 18, 1862.[23] The command was made up principally of lumbermen and coal miners from the surrounding mountains of Luzerne, Susquehanna, Wyoming, and Lycoming counties, many of whom had never before been more than a few miles from home. They had signed up because they had been promised a $60 bounty for enlisting—$10 when they were sworn in, and $50 after their initial training.[24] Lured in by the prospect of quick cash and a short war, many of these men would pay for their naiveté with their lives less than a year later and fewer than 100 miles from home.

Initial drill instruction was commenced in July 1862 at Camp Luzerne in Kingston, Pennsylvania, one of the many camps established in the Keystone State. During the summer and fall, the officers instructed the men on the basics of military life. Spirits were high when the regiment broke camp four months later and traveled to Harrisburg where they were armed with Enfield rifles.[25] On November 7, the regiment left Pennsylvania for the defenses of Washington.

The 143rd Pennsylvania arrived in Washington on November 11 and were initially placed under the command of General Casey.[26] The remainder of the winter was spent assisting in the construction of Fort Slocum on the northern fringes of Washington, D.C. When not engaged in "fatigue duty upon the fortifications," the enlisted men of the regiment were drilled in the manual of arms while the officers attended military schools.[27] During this time, the poor sanitation conditions around Washington resulted in the death of many of the Pennsylvanians.

23. Samuel P. Bates, *Martial Deeds of Pennsylvania*. Philadelphia, 1875; Samuel P. Bates, *History of the Pennsylvania Volunteers*, 4: 487; George B. Kulp, *Families of the Wyoming Valley. Biographical, Genealogical, and Historical Sketches of the Bench and Bar of Luzerne County, Pennsylvania*, 2 Vols. (Wilkes-Barre, Pennsylvania, 1885), 1: 34.

24. Letter to the Editor, *Daily Record of the Times* (Wilkes Barre, Pennsylvania), July 16, 1875. In this letter the men of Company D complained that they had never received a cent of the bounty they had been promised.

25. Samuel P. Bates, *History of the Pennsylvania Volunteers*, 4: 487.

26. Thomas Chamberlin, *History of the One Hundred Fiftieth Pennsylvania*, 49.

27. Ibid., 487. Pennsylvania Gettysburg Battlefield Commission, *Pennsylvania at Gettysburg: Ceremonies at the Dedication of the Monuments Erected by the Commonwealth of Pennsylvania to Mark the Positions of the Pennsylvania Commands Engaged in the Battle*, John P. Nicholson, ed., 2: 695 (Harrisburg, Pennsylvania: W.S. Ray, State Printer, 1904).

On February 17, 1863, the regiment was ordered forward to Belle Plain, Virginia, where it was assigned to Colonel Roy Stone's Bucktail brigade. The 149th and 150th Pennsylvania, having been previously assigned to the brigade, were sometimes less than cordial with the newly acquired regiment and frequently conveyed the worst duties to the newcomers.[28] Having spent the winter together, the men of the 149th and 150th Pennsylvania had built a strong bond. While the officers of the three regiments were cordial to each other, the men had developed a fierce pride at having been recruited specifically into the Bucktails. The 143rd Pennsylvania had been assigned merely to fill out the command. As a result, they were seen as outsiders. The friction which developed would outlast the war.

28. Richard Sauers, *Advance the Colors; Pennsylvania Civil War Battle Flags.* (Harrisburg: Pennsylvania Capitol Preservation Committee), 2: 434.

Chapter 2

SPRING 1863

"...in excellent spirits and condition."

THE NEWLY ORGANIZED Bucktails accompanied General Joseph Hooker's Army of the Potomac when it crossed the Rappahannock and engaged Robert E. Lee at Chancellorsville. Having yet to see combat, it was surely a sobering sight for the men of Stone's brigade when they approached the battlefield around midnight on May 2, 1863, and passed the horribly mangled bodies of their dead and wounded comrades still littering the ground from the day's action.[29] Upon reaching the Chancellorsville turnpike, the Bucktails were directed to the left and marched toward the Chancellor House. During the night, the 150th Pennsylvania threw out skirmishers about two hundred yards to their front. Because of the darkness, the 150th's skirmishers were instructed to role up one sleeve of their blouse thus exposing one arm and providing a unique source of identification.[30] Aside from skirmish duty, the remainder of the night passed without incident, though few probably got much rest. One veteran recalled that the only other memorable event that night was the annoying song of some hungry mules.[31]

Positioned on the far right of Hooker's command overlooking Hunting Creek, the brigade saw little action during the battle. When the Rebels attacked early on the morning of May 3, the Pennsylvanians were instructed to throw up strong breastworks. This done, the First Corps watched as the fighting raged off to their left. Lieutenant Colonel Huidekoper was instructed to take out a

29. Samuel P. Bates, *History of the Pennsylvania Volunteers*, 4: 487-488.
30. Thomas Chamberlin, *History of the One Hundred Fiftieth Pennsylvania*, 89.
31. John P. Nicholson, *Pennsylvania at Gettysburg*, 2: 695.

party of skirmishers. He had advanced nearly half a mile when they began to receive fire from the Rebels. Despite this, the Bucktails stuck to their work and were able to capture a number of prisoners throughout the day.[32] The brigade had not yet been attacked when the fighting sputtered out around noon.

At 5 P.M. on the following day, May 4, the Bucktails were assigned to scout the rear of the enemy's position which was completed without incident. Early on the afternoon of May 6, the return march was begun. The Second Brigade traveled by way of White Oak Church and Belle Plain before going into camp about two miles from the Rappahannock near Pollock's Mill two days later.[33] Stone recalled that, "[I had] more men for duty and more arms than when the campaign commenced, and in excellent spirits and condition."[34]

The Federal army was camped outside Falmouth when in mid-June the brigade received its orders to march. In an effort to relieve Grant's siege of Vicksburg and to allow Virginia farmers an unmolested growing season, the Army of Northern Virginia had begun to move north with the intention of invading Pennsylvania. The enlisted soldiers were not made aware of their destination or purpose, but it was clear to them that they were headed north, as they moved through Bealton Station and along the Orange and Alexandria Railroad. Hooker's route kept the Federal army east of the Shenandoah, careful to stay between the advancing Rebels and Washington. Near Elk Church the brigade witnessed the execution of a deserter who, having been shot, was buried alongside the road.[35] The march through Virginia and Maryland was, "one of the most torturous . . . on record. The heat of the sun was withering. Not a breath of air stirred the leaves; the dust rose like a white cloud . . . not a drop of water was to be had . . . . "[36]

William Wright of Company I, 149th Pennsylvania, vividly recalled the difficulties of the march:

We marched all day without stopping to get water or cook coffee until sundown. The sun was awful hot and

---

32. Thomas Chamberlin, *History of the One Hundred Fiftieth Pennsylvania*, 90.
33. Ibid., 99; Bates, *History of the Pennsylvania Volunteers*, 4: 488.
34. Ibid., 4: 612.
35. Thomas Chamberlin, *History of the One Hundred Fiftieth Pennsylvania*, 108.
36. Ibid., 109.

dust so mouth deep we nearly starved for water. I was so sore and tired that I could scarcely get one foot before the other. Several of the boys fell out of the line just as we halted for the night. Colonel Dwight, who was so drunk that he could scarcely sit on his horse ordered 100 of our regiment on picket. I had to go on picket. I was obliged to use my gun in place of a cane for I couldn't walk without support . . . That night, if it had been the Lord's will, I would have welcomed death in preference to army life.[37]

On the morning of June 15, the Bucktails reached Centreville and encamped near "two beautiful springs, which, after the trials of the three-days' march, were more precious than gold."[38] During the last few days of June, as the Bucktails approached Pennsylvania, the mood of the officers grew more serious. On June 21, Adjutant Ashurst of the 150th Pennsylvania wrote, "We are under orders to be ready to march at any moment."[39] Avery Harris of the 143rd Pennsylvania described the mood of the officers as, "grave and quiet and very reticent and apparently more thoughtful."[40]

The Federals crossed the Potomac on June 27, 1863, and camped near Middletown, Maryland, throwing out a strong picket line for the night. Later that evening while Charley Wilson of the 143rd Pennsylvania stood on the picket line, he noticed a small group of young women approaching from the direction of a nearby church. Though obviously returning home from Sunday school, Wilson advised them that they could not pass. Some of the young ladies, alarmed at their situation, began to cry. Lonely, as most infantrymen are when far from home, he devised a plan where all could benefit. Wilson told them that they could pass but only if each one gave him a kiss. This they did, and each was permitted to return home without further hindrance.[41]

---

37. Richard Matthews, *The 149th Pennsylvania*, 68-69.
38. Thomas Chamberlin, *History of the One Hundred and Fiftieth Regiment Pennsylvania Volunteers* (Philadelphia, 1905), 110.
39. Ibid., 113.
40. Avery Harris Journal, USAMHI, Copy GNMP.
41. Simon Hubler Account, Brake Collection, USAMHI, Copy GNMP. Charles Wilson does not appear on the roster for the 143rd Pennsylvania. There was a Charles Williams from Luzerne County in Company D and a William Wilson in Company K. It is likely that Hubler was referring to one of these men when he related this episode, but the passage of 49 years had clouded his recollection of his comrade's name.

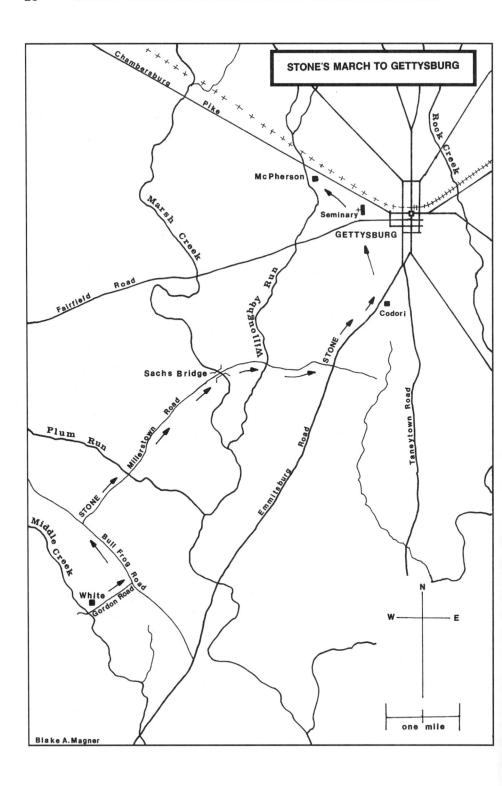

Later that night, two different young ladies approached the line and in a gracious display of Maryland generosity, offered to mail the men's letters home. The opportunity was quickly seized and before long the ladies had a large supply of letters to take with them. Every letter was properly delivered.[42]

On June 29, First Corps marched to Frederick, Maryland, and camped in the western suburbs, picketing the roads to the north-west. The night passed without incident and dawn saw the men back on their feet; their destination was Emmitsburg. After a long and arduous march, First Corps passed through Emmitsburg and was ordered to bivouac on the heights north of town. Presumably this position had been identified by General John Reynolds to be the most suitable for defense. The enemy had been reported in strength at Fairfield and General Reynolds was taking no chances.[43]

Tuesday, June 30, the Second Brigade marched a short distance north on the Middle Creek Road, eventually turning east on Gordon Road and camping for the night on the Samuel White farm.[44] Skirmishers were undoubtedly thrown out to the north and the area of Fairfield where the enemy had earlier been engaged.

It was here, after the replacement of Joseph Hooker with Major General George Gordon Meade on June 28, that Reynolds was instructed to retake command of the left wing of the army, then consisting of the First, Eleventh, and Third Corps. This promoted Abner Doubleday, the corps' senior division commander, to command of First Corps. Doubleday filled the vacant Third Division command with Brigadier General Thomas A. Rowley and he in turn delegated command of the First Brigade to Colonel Chapman Biddle of the 121st Pennsylvania.[45]

During the night of June 30, a practical joker spread the news that the Mother Superior of the local convent had invited all the commissioned officers to a reception where, of course, suitable refreshments would be served. Most were adept enough to recog-

---

42. Ibid. It is interesting to note that most of these letters were without postage and that these kind young ladies spent their own money to make sure these letters got to the appropriate destination.

43. United States War Department, *The War of the Rebellion: A Compilation of the Official Records of the Union and Confederate Armies*, 70 vols. In 128 parts (Washington, D.C.: Government Printing Office, 1880-1901), Series 1, Vol. XXVII, pt. 1, p. 243. (Hereafter cited as *O.R.* All subsequent references are from Series 1.)

44. Most accounts indicate that the division was camped in the area of Marsh Creek, however, investigations into local claims filed by Tim Smith have, for the first time, pinpointed the actual location of Stone's camp to be on the Samuel White farm.

45. *O.R.*, Vol. XXVII, pt. 1, p. 244.

nize the absurdity of the story; but a few were foolish enough to pay a visit to the convent which they found dark and quiet.[46] That night, the men of the Bucktail brigade slept under a full moon unaware that the events of tomorrow would write their names indelibly in American history.[47]

---

46. Thomas Chamberlin, *History of the One Hundred Fiftieth Pennsylvania*, 116.

47. Thomas L. Elmore, "A Meteorological and Astronomical Chronology of the Gettysburg Campaign." *Gettysburg Magazine*, Morningside Press, July 1995, 13: 10.

Chapter 3

THE MANOR OF MASKE

A Pre-battle History of the McPherson Farm

DURING THE LATE MORNING and afternoon of July 1, 1863, the Pennsylvania Bucktails fought tenaciously for possession of a 110-acre farm just west of Gettysburg, Pennsylvania. Afterward, the farm, owned by Edward McPherson, Chief Clerk of the House of Representatives, would become forever inextricably associated with the First Day's fight of the battle of Gettysburg. Since then, the "McPherson Farm," much like the Peach Orchard and the Wheatfield, has conjured images of heroic struggles and ghastly casualties.

The portion of the battlefield we now know as the McPherson Farm was originally part of a huge land grant issued to William Penn by King Charles II of England in 1681. Penn would later name his roughly 45,000 square miles of land, Pennsylvania or "Penn's Woods." In the early eighteenth century, the ground where the McPherson Farm now stands was settled by Scotch-Irish immigrants who called it the Marsh Creek Settlement. Later, in 1741, William Penn's sons set aside some 43,500 acres of land in Pennsylvania and called it the Manor of Maske. On May 30, 1765, the Penn family issued a warrant to Robert Stewart for 121 acres of land in Cumberland Township, York County, making Stewart the farm's first recorded owner.[48]

Sometime before 1798, the land was transferred to its second recorded owner, William Breadon. At the time of the 1798 tax assess-

---

48. Timothy H. Smith, *The Story of Lee's Headquarters* (Gettysburg, 1995), 2; Robert L. Bloom, *A History of Adams County, Pennsylvania 1700-1990* (Gettysburg, 1992), 5-6; Charles H. Glatfelter and Arthur Weaner, *The Manor of Maske: Its History and Individual Properties* (Biglerville, 1992), 33.

ment, Breadon was farming 118 acres east of Willoughby Run. Upon occupying a new tract of land, farmers would usually build a small, temporary home for their family, but the majority of their exertions went toward constructing a sturdy, permanent barn to house their livestock. Once the farmers' sources of income (horses, cattle, harvested crops) were protected from the elements, they could enlarge and modify the temporary living quarters. Such was the case with the Breadon family. The tax assessment of 1797 described a 20-foot by 18-foot, one-story log dwelling with three windows and an unfinished 24-foot by 16-foot fieldstone addition. A 50-foot by 17-foot log barn stood just northwest of the house.[49] The 1800 census indicated a total of eight people living at the house: Breadon, his wife, a son, and five daughters.[50]

According to the tax records, Breadon entered the area after 1790 and was still completing his home in 1798 when the property was assessed. In 1802, he sold the farm, then nearly 127 acres, and moved from the area.[51] The Reverend David McConaughy purchased the farm that year and began working the land.[52] In 1809, a pike that would bisect his land was proposed, starting in Gettysburg and connecting Cashtown and Chambersburg. This pike would eventually become known as the Cashtown or Chambersburg Turnpike. Prior to its construction, no road ran westward from the town of Gettysburg. At the time however, the Hagerstown Road ran southwest from town and the Mummasburg Road jogged off to the northwest. It is said that an old dirt road connected these two roads and ran from the Hagerstown Road at its intersection with Seminary Ridge northwest in the direction of the Upper Marsh Creek Presbyterian Graveyard. Apparently it went "directly by the old stone building, then owned by Rev. Mr. McConaughy . . . and up through the farms west of it . . . ."[53] Breadon's and now McConaughy's home faced eastward toward this road. McConaughy was irate about the new pike crossing his

49. Kathleen R. Georg, *Edward McPherson Farm: Historical Study*, GNMP, October 14, 1977.
50. 1800 U.S. Census for Pennsylvania, National Archives, Microfilm Copy, GNMP.
51. Kathleen R. Georg, *Edward McPherson Farm: Historical Study*, GNMP. Breadon does not appear on the 1790 tax rolls so we can assume that he and his family arrived after that year. Considering that the house was not yet complete in 1798, we can further assume that he and his family may not have arrived until 1795 or 1796.
52. It was McConaughy's son David who became instrumental in the development of the Gettysburg National Cemetery and the Gettysburg Battlefield Memorial Association. David purchased East Cemetery Hill and Little Round Top within weeks of the battle.
53. Edward McPherson, "Local History," *Star and Sentinel,*" May 14, 1895.

land and he petitioned the courts for damages as a result of its inconvenience. He claimed that the pike took away over two thousand linear feet of his land and changed the character of his home by "compelling the abandonment of the old dirt road, or bringing his barn to the front and throwing his house to the rear, and of obliging him to supply a new approach to the highway." For his trouble he received $100.[54]

Sometime during McConaughy's ownership, the original log barn built by Breadon was replaced by the stone bank barn that existed at the time of the battle of Gettysburg. When an owner modified his property, the tax assessor typically made note of it in the tax records for the year when the alteration occurred. Since no record can be found regarding the construction of the new barn and because tax records are missing for the years 1812-1823, we can assume that it occurred sometime during those eleven years.[55] It is reasonable to assume that McConaughy may have accrued sufficient funds by this time to replace the old log barn with a more substantial stone one.

Though he was clearly legally and financially committed to the farm, McConaughy never actually lived or worked on it. McConaughy was an absentee landlord who may have assigned the actual labor to his two black slaves. Despite its productivity, in 1827 Reverend McConaughy retired and sold the farm, then 110 acres (17 had been sold off previously to Abraham Spangler), to a group of three investors—David Ziegler, Michael C. Clarkson, and John L. Fuller.[56]

For a brief period, the three men managed the farm while trying to find a buyer. Eventually, Ziegler and Fuller sold their shares to Clarkson who continued to maintain the land. Clarkson, like McConaughy before him, was an absentee landlord living in Gettysburg and renting the land to tenants. During the 1830s, Clarkson's fame and wealth grew exponentially. He was elected to the borough council in 1834 and to the burgess of Gettysburg in 1839. It seems, however, that he had a reversal of fortune in the mid-1840s when he was ordered to sell off some property to pay an $1,800 debt. A few months passed without any buyers and in early

---

54. Kathleen R. Georg, *Edward McPherson Farm: Historical Study*, GNMP.

55. Ibid.

56. Ibid.; Tax Records, Cumberland Township, 1828-1832, Adams County Historical Society.

1846 the farm was seized and sold at auction. John B. McPherson was the high bidder at $2,215, which was more than enough to pay off Clarkson's debt.[57]

Soon after the sale of the farm, Clarkson disappeared from Gettysburg. Perhaps he and his family could not endure the humiliation of their financial hardship and chose to relocate to an area where no one knew their names.[58]

Clarkson, it seems, never improved on the farm in the time of his ownership. His greatest contribution to the record of the farm may have been in its auction, since the deed of sale lists the structures present on the property in 1845. It lists, "a one and one half story dwelling house, Bank barn, Wagon Shed and other outbuilding, with a well of water and an orchard of Fruit Trees . . . ."[59] This clearly indicates that the house built by Breadon in 1798 was still standing and that the structures that show up in the 1863 Brady photograph (the wagon shed, corn crib, house, and stone barn) were all there in 1845 at the time of the sale.[60]

John B. McPherson, who owned the farm for 22 years, was a descendent of Robert McPherson, who had settled the area in 1738 and was therefore a member of the "First Families of Adams County." John McPherson had achieved considerable local fame by the time he purchased the farm in 1845. He was regularly elected to the borough council, was a trustee for Pennsylvania College, and had worked for the Bank of Gettysburg since it was founded in 1814. His grandfather, Robert McPherson Jr., had served as a captain in the Seven Years War and as a colonel during the American Revolution. In 1776, he served as a delegate to the Constitutional Convention. John McPherson, father of John B., was a lieutenant during the Revolution and was later a state assemblyman. John B. McPherson was a successful investor, having owned numerous properties in and around Gettysburg. The farm was his first attempt at being an absentee farmer. In 1858, the year of John B. McPherson's death, the tenant was listed as C. Eckert. The heir to McPherson's possessions was his 28-year-old son, Edward.[61]

57. Kathleen R. Georg, *Edward McPherson Farm: Historical Study*, GNMP.
58. Ibid.
59. Ibid; Deedbook Z, p. 466, Adams County Courthouse.
60. Ibid.
61. Frank R. Metzger, *The Honorable Edward McPherson, Citizen of Gettysburg*, Unpublished, May, 1933, Adams County Historical Society.

Edward McPherson was brought up a proud Scotsman. He was educated at Pennsylvania College and graduated at the top of his class in 1848. From there he went on to study law, eventually entering the Lancaster law practice of Thaddeus Stevens. He learned a great deal from Stevens who acted as McPherson's mentor. As their friendship developed, Stevens's political beliefs soon became his own. The influence that Stevens had over McPherson would affect many of his future career decisions.[62]

Later, McPherson developed an illness that required his resignation from the law firm. While recovering in Harrisburg, McPherson accepted the first of many jobs in journalism. In the years that followed, Edward McPherson worked as a reporter and editor for a number of papers in the Harrisburg, Lancaster, and Pittsburgh areas eventually returning to Gettysburg in 1856. Here his journalism career temporarily ceased—perhaps due to pressure from his father who would have preferred a politician son to a newspaperman. In 1858 and 1860, Edward was elected to Congress but lost the election in 1862 because of the addition of the hostile Bedford County to his Congressional District. Thaddeus Stevens, a Radical Republican, used his considerable influence to get his former law partner appointed to the position of Chief Clerk of the House of Representatives, a position McPherson held during 1863–1877, 1881–1883, and 1889–1891, a total of 18 years. McPherson's sense of obligation to Stevens was evident and resulted in his being less than unbiased.[63]

Following Lincoln's assassination, President Andrew Johnson adopted Lincoln's policy of "malice toward none" when he graciously allowed the former Confederate states which had accepted the Thirteenth Amendment to elect representatives to Congress. Stevens, however, did not share the president's benevolent sentiments and arranged with McPherson to omit from the roll the names of the newly elected representatives. Steven's vengeance toward the South set the stage for Radical Reconstruction.[64]

His growing political career kept McPherson away from Gettysburg for long periods of time. The farm needed constant attention and would therefore require a tenant.[65]

---

62. Ibid.
63. Ibid. Dumas Malone, *Dictionary of American Biography* (New York, 1946), 11: 159-160.
64. Kathleen R. Georg, *Edward McPherson Farm: Historical Study*, GNMP.
65. Ibid.

John T. Slentz applied for and became McPherson's new tenant. The 1860 census showed that John Slentz, aged 32, lived there with his wife Eliza, who was 27, and their three children, aged eight, six, and one. About 70 years later, Sarah (one year old in 1860) remembered that in the southern section of the house, made of logs, were a kitchen and dining room on the first floor and two bedrooms on the second floor while the northern section, made of stone, consisted of a bedroom and parlor on the first floor and two additional bedrooms on the second floor. She also recalled that to move from the log section into the stone section required climbing two steps.[66]

With Edward McPherson away in Washington, John Slentz was free to farm the property unmolested by his landlord. By the time war reached south-central Pennsylvania in July 1863, Slentz had accumulated considerable wealth and had amassed three cows, six calves, four horses, four hogs, three turkeys, and some forty chickens. Ninety-five of his acres were planted in wheat, corn, oats, and grass. The remainder, about 30 acres, was woodland and pasture for his livestock. Around the house was a young orchard for the purposes of cooking and preserving. Indeed, until late June 1863, farming was very profitable for the Slentzes.[67]

In the early summer of 1863, Gettysburg residents followed closely in the *Gettysburg Compiler* and the *Star and Sentinel* the advance of Robert E. Lee's Army of Northern Virginia. The first clash with Jubal Early on June 26 signaled the beginning of difficult times for the residents of the town.[68]

On the morning of June 30, the Rebel brigade of Johnston Pettigrew advanced eastward on the Chambersburg Pike on its way to Gettysburg to relieve the town of any remaining supplies. The Confederates passed through the farm that morning and probably questioned Slentz about Federals in the vicinity. Arriving on Seminary Ridge, the Rebels could see the approach of John Buford's two brigades from the south and prudently withdrew, not knowing the Federal strength. The events of the next day would change forever the face of the farm and would record its name in the annals of American history.

66. Ibid.
67. Ibid.
68. Michael Jacobs, *Notes on the Rebel Invasion of Maryland and Pennsylvania and the Battle of Gettysburg, July 1, 2nd, and 3rd, 1863*, (Philadelphia, 1864), 21.

Chapter 4

STONE TAKES POSITION ON THE MCPHERSON FARM

"This day, go in for Pennsylvania."

THE WEATHER ON the morning of July 1, 1863, indicated that it was to be a typical summer day in south-central Pennsylvania. The sun rose at 4:35 A.M. and a light rain fell between 6:00 and 8:00 A.M. The sun finally broke through around 9:00 A.M. and the temperature quickly climbed.[69] Lieutenant Colonel Henry S. Huidekoper of the 150th Pennsylvania described that it soon ". . . became sultry beyond measure."[70] Federal General John Reynolds sent for General Abner Doubleday around 6:00 A.M. to discuss the latest reports received from General George Gordon Meade and his cavalry regarding the last known movements of the Rebels. It was clear that the enemy was concentrating in the direction of Gettysburg. Federal Brigadier General John Buford, commanding the First Cavalry Division, was already engaged with elements of Confederate Lieutenant General Ambrose P. Hill's Corps on the western outskirts of the town. Buford had previously identified these ridges as necessary to defend if this critical crossroads town were to be occupied by the Federal army and a general battle fought. John Reynolds, while not lacking faith in Buford, was a hands-on general; he needed to see and feel the fight to anticipate its movement. Reynolds advised Doubleday that James S. Wadsworth's division

---

69. The rest of the day would be hot and humid. Thomas L. Elmore, "A Meteorological and Astronomical Chronology of the Gettysburg Campaign," *Gettysburg Magazine*, (Morningside Press, July 1995), 13: 10
70. Henry S. Huidekoper, A Short Story of the First Day's Fight at Gettysburg. Reprinted in *Gettysburg Sources* (Baltimore, 1986), 1: 17.

along with Captain James Hall's 2nd Maine Battery had already been ordered up to Buford's assistance and that he was going to ride on ahead to get a better look at the situation. His last order to Doubleday was to call in his pickets, assemble the remainder of the corps, and to join him in Gettysburg "as soon as possible." With that, Reynolds rode off, not knowing that it would be the last time the two would meet.[71]

Simon Hubler of Company I, 143rd Pennsylvania, woke up hungry that morning. Though he carried three days' rations issued the previous day,[72] he had a craving for something fresh. He thought if he were quick, he could forage in the nearby countryside and return to his regiment before anyone noticed he was gone. As luck would have it, however, Doubleday's order to assemble and move out was received while Hubler was still out scrounging. Returning in a misty rain, he found the entire brigade gone. All that was left was his rifle and blanket. In the distance he could hear the booming of Lieutenant John H. Calef's Battery A, 2nd U.S. Artillery's six 3-inch rifles, already engaged west of Gettysburg. With alacrity he set off in pursuit of his company.[73]

It took nearly an hour and a half for Doubleday to call in his pickets, break camp, and assemble the men. As a result, Wadsworth's troops arrived on the field far in advance of the rest of the corps. Drawing near the town around 10:00 A.M., having ridden forward and overtaken Wadsworth's troops, Doubleday was assigned to oversee Brigadier General Solomon Meredith's Iron Brigade which was already deployed south of the Chambersburg Pike facing west. Meanwhile, north of the pike, Wadsworth directed Brigadier General Lysander Cutler's brigade into position. In the interim between his arrival and that of his division, Doubleday was forced to fight a pitched battle with Henry Heth's division of Hill's Corps deployed on the ridge opposite his position. The outcome of this initial phase of fighting on July 1 appeared doubtful. Having lost John Reynolds to a fatal head wound early in the fight before Reynolds could disclose his plans to anyone, Doubleday was left to postulate

---

71. Ibid., 244; Abner Doubleday, *Chancellorsville and Gettysburg* (New York, 1882), 124-125. In his official report of the battle, Doubleday cited the time of his meeting with Reynolds as "between 7 and 8 o'clock." In his book, *Chancellorsville and Gettysburg*, published in 1882, he would remember this time as "six o'clock in the morning."
72. Avery Harris Journal, Copy GNMP.
73. Simon Hubler Account, Brake Collection, USAMHI, Copy GNMP. The brigade moved out between 8 A.M. and 9 A.M.

about his overall strategy. First Lieutenant Jacob F. Slagle of Company D, 149th Pennsylvania, overheard a conversation upon Doubleday's arrival on the field: " . . . he said all he could do was fight until he got sufficient information to form his own plan."[74] John Reynolds had felt a momentous responsibility to defend this town. With that in mind, Doubleday fought his First Division with an aptitude some doubted he had.[75] Evidence of the ferocity of the opening hours of the battle could be seen strewn about the field. Lieutenant John Calef related that, "the field . . . presented a true battle picture, such as one sees occasionally portrayed on canvas, but which, seen in all the horrors of its reality, can never be effaced from the memory."[76]

By 11:30 A.M., as General T. A. Rowley's division approached the field, McPherson's Ridge was again entirely in the hands of the Federals who had fought so desperately to retain it. Confederate Major General Henry Heth had been forced to withdraw his two brigades under Brigadier Generals James J. Archer and Joseph R. Davis back across Willoughby Run to Herr Ridge, a mile distant. The two commands had suffered intensely at the hands of Wadsworth's First Division and a reorganization was in order. Archer, on the right, had been overwhelmed by superior numbers and by a costly enfilade fire pumped into his right flank by the men of the Iron Brigade. Archer himself had been captured during the clash. Joe Davis had made fair progress early on by forcing Cutler to retire, which resulted in the abandonment of the 147th New York and the overrunning of one of Hall's unsupported guns. The placement of Hall's guns was controversial. In his anxiety to cover his front, Wadsworth had placed them in an exposed position. In his diary, Colonel Charles S. Wainwright, commanding the First Corps artillery, claimed that Wadsworth kept interfering with the proper placement of his guns:

I did not like this advanced position at all, its right flank being exposed to a high ridge to the north, and

74. Letter of Jacob F. Slagle to his Brother, September 13, 1863, Copy GNMP.

75. Allen Nevins, *Diary of Battle*, 233. Colonel Wainwright recorded that, "I had no confidence in Doubleday, and felt that he would be a weak reed to lean upon . . . ."

76. O.R., Vol. XXVII, pt. 1, pp. 244, 266. Doubleday, *Chancellorsville and Gettysburg*, 132; George Gordon Meade, *Life and Letters of George G. Meade* (New York, 1913), 2: 349; John Calef, *Gettysburg Notes: The Opening Gun*, Journal of the Military Service Institution of the United States, 1907, 40: 50.

approached by a number of ravines which afforded excellent cover to an attacking party. General Wadsworth had ordered Hall back again, but I took the responsibility of forbidding him to put his battery there until I knew there were troops to cover his right flank . . . .[77]

Doubleday arrived on the right just in time to witness these events and to order a charge by the 6th Wisconsin, until then held in reserve near the Lutheran Theological Seminary. The subsequent fight for the Railroad Cut resulted in the recapture of Hall's piece and the nabbing of over 200 Mississippians and North Carolinians. Now badly bloodied, both Rebel brigades fell back across McPherson's Ridge. The Confederates had been considerably reduced in strength and were badly demoralized. The relative safety afforded by this withdrawal to Herr Ridge enabled Heth to reform his troops and to bring up some guns for another try at the Federals.[78]

By this time General Reynolds was dead, struck in the back of the head by a Confederate minie ball delivered by one of Archer's men advancing through Herbst Woods. By virtue of his seniority, Major General Oliver O. Howard of the Eleventh Corps assumed command of the field from Doubleday when he arrived in Gettysburg around 10:30 A.M. Doubleday remained in command of First Corps and continued to direct them through the morning while Howard reconnoitered the area and developed a plan of defense.[79] Howard immediately recognized the importance of Cemetery Hill and decided to place Brigadier General Adolph von Steinwehr's Second Division along with three batteries under Major Thomas Osborn there in reserve. When Major General Carl Schurz of the Third Division arrived around 1:00 P.M., Howard turned over command of the Eleventh Corps to Schurz and rode forward to look over the First Corps position west of town.[80]

South of Gettysburg the Bucktails, broiling in the hot Pennsylvania sun and dripping with sweat, hurried toward the sound of battle. Sergeant Shafer of Company I, 143rd Pennsylvania,

---

77. Allen Nevins, *Diary of Battle*, 235.
78. O.R., Vol. XXVII, pt. 1, p. 245.
79. Edwin B. Coddington, *The Gettysburg Campaign: A Study in Command* (New York, 1963), 278-279.
80. Ibid., 282.

remembered that the regiment had marched about "3 miles at double-time and the balance at double-quick." Others recalled traveling "so fast I could not keep up" and "at a very rapid rate, I had to fall out." Captain William P. Dougal of Company D, 150th Pennsylvania, also found the pace too great and was forced to ask for permission to drop out. Due to his immense size, he was given this permission but with the stipulation that he gather up stragglers and bring them to the front.[81]

Evidence suggests that the brigade moved from the Samuel White farm, where they had spent the night, to the Bull Frog Road, and then east on the Millerstown Road (now Pumping Station Road), crossed Sachs covered bridge, and arrived at the Millerstown Road intersection with the Emmittsburg Road at the Peach Orchard.[82] From there they followed the Emmittsburg Road north toward Gettysburg, leaving the road just south of the Codori farm and advancing north across the intervening fields toward the Lutheran Theological Seminary visible in the distance.[83]

Nearing the fighting, the men of the Second Brigade came across five small children mounted on a fatigued horse and in an obvious search for safety. "My God, they are driving people from their homes," shouted one of the Bucktails. Further on, Doubleday approached them on horseback. "What command is this?" he demanded. "The Pennsylvania Brigade," the men answered. Inspiring his troops forward, Doubleday cried, "This day, go in for Pennsylvania." Along with cheers from the ranks came the roar of "We have come to stay!" Before the general rode off he exclaimed, "Hold them boys when you get there." Roused by the exchange, one man shouted back, "If we can't hold them, where can you get men that can?"[84]

Upon approaching the Seminary, Colonel Edmund L. Dana of the 143rd Pennsylvania became aware that they were about to be thrust into a raging battle. He halted and ordered the regiment to

---

81. Thomas Chamberlin, *History of the One Hundred and Fiftieth Pennsylvania*, 118. Dougal did eventually bring up the stragglers later in the morning and was himself wounded later in the day.

82. August 7, 1999, interview with Tim Smith relative to Stone's route of march, July 1, 1863.

83. Henry Huidekoper, *A Short Story of the First Day's Fight at Gettysburg*, 19; "Gettysburg Reminiscences," *National Tribune*, October 20, 1898. Copy GNMP; William R. Ramsey to J.H. Bassler, August 3, 1906, Bassler Ramsey Collection, USAMHI. Copy GNMP. According to Sergeant Shafer the regiment marched 5 miles that morning.

84. Henry Huidekoper, *A Short Story of the First Day's Fight at Gettysburg*, 19; Patrick DeLacy, "Capt. DeLacy Describes Gettysburg Battle," *The Scranton Truth*, 1913. DeLacy was a sergeant in Company A, 143rd Pennsylvania, at the time of the battle.

deposit their blankets and knapsacks in a pile, leaving a single man to guard them. Isaac B. Noecker of Company C, 149th Pennsylvania, wrote home to his local newspaper that, " . . . when we reached a corn field . . . we were halted and ordered to unsling knapsacks . . . ."[85] Corporal Simon Hubler remembered that, "we saw nothing of these knapsacks until after the battle when we discovered that they had been filled with sand by the Rebels and had been used by them as a breastwork."[86] Surely tensions were high as the brigade crested Seminary Ridge and witnessed first hand the sights and sounds of the battlefield. Sergeant DeLacy of Company I, 143rd Pennsylvania, remembered that, "our boys were itching to get into the struggle."[87] To his left front across the valley, Corporal Sanford N. Boyden of Company A, 149th Pennsylvania, could see the Iron Brigade engaged with Archer in Herbst Woods: "[We] passed over Seminary Ridge and found the Iron Brigade of the 1st Division in the woods near Willoughby Run . . . ."[88]

On the right, Cutler had withdrawn his troops to the safety of the wooded slope of Oak Ridge to regroup. This exposed Meredith's unprotected right flank. Doubleday, who had just received orders from the ranking Howard to "hold Seminary Hill [Ridge] at all hazards," threw Stone's brigade forward into the gap. He then placed Biddle's brigade in support of Meredith and Stone, giving General Rowley "charge of this part of the line."[89] General Robinson's division was ordered to remain at the Seminary in reserve and to fortify the position in the event that McPherson's Ridge was overrun. According to Doubleday, "toward the close of the action this defense, weak and imperfect as it was, proved to be of great service."[90] Company D of the 149th Pennsylvania was left on Seminary Ridge in its role as headquarters guard. Their line extended from south of the Seminary to the Fairfield Road.

To some it may have seemed strange that Doubleday spent so much time and effort placing the two brigades of Rowley's division.

---

85. O.R., Vol. XXVII, pt. 1, p. 334. Isaac B. Noecker letter to the Lebanon *Courier*, July 9, 1863.
86. Simon Hubler Account.
87. Patrick DeLacy, "Capt. DeLacy Describes Gettysburg Battle."
88. Letter from Corporal Sanford N. Boyden, Company A, 149th PVI to Captain R. E. Gamble. March 15, 1906. Copy GNMP. This quote clearly illustrates how much less dense Herbst Woods was in 1863 compared to modern day. At the time, grazing animals had cleared out the underlying brush making it possible to see through the woods to the western edge. Today it is impossible to see more than a few yards into the woods let alone all the way to Willoughby Run. Nicholson, *Pennsylvania at Gettysburg*, 2: 738.
89. O.R., Vol. XXVII, pt. 1, p. 247.
90. Ibid., Doubleday, *Chancellorsville and Gettysburg*, 136.

Rowley was not particularly liked nor trusted by his peers.[91] His military career was unremarkable and he had been promoted to command of the division on the eve of the battle. These obstacles aside, Rowley was in the difficult position of commanding two brigades positioned nearly a quarter of a mile apart. If this were not enough, Rowley made matters worse for himself by becoming drunk during the battle. It is clear through numerous reports that he exercised little control over Biddle's brigade and is not known to have communicated with nor visited Stone's brigade at all during the conflict. His erratic behavior did not go unnoticed. Colonel Theodore Gates of the 151st Pennsylvania (Biddle's brigade) reported that, "During the fighting on the first day the General commanding the division was hardly competent to judge correctly the condition of things, or to know what transpired on the field."[92] Colonel Wainwright complained about Rowley's inability to manage the troops supporting his guns. "A brigade [Biddle's] of the Third Division sent to support the battery persisted in getting in front—that being its commander's idea of supporting . . . There was not a shadow of a chance of our holding this ridge even had our Third Division commanders had any idea what to do with their men, which they had not." Later in the day, when Rowley finally became too disorderly to responsibly command his troops, he was placed under arrest and escorted from the field at the point of a bayonet.[93]

The rest of Stone's brigade, some 1,300 strong,[94] moved forward, colors unfurled, and occupied the area of McPherson's Ridge between the northern edge of Herbst Woods and the Chambersburg Pike. In doing so, Stone had the foresight to keep the brigade posted on the eastern slope of the ridge, which provided some cover and concealment from the Rebels in the swale beyond. Colonel Dana of the 143rd Pennsylvania made note of the time: "[The] engagement opened at a quarter before 12m."[95]

Arriving at the McPherson Farm, Stone began directing his command into position. On the left between Herbst Woods and the McPherson house, he placed the 150th Pennsylvania (nine compa-

91. Allen Nevins, A Diary of Battle, 237.
92. David Martin, Gettysburg July 1 (Conshohocken, 1995), 180-181.
93. Lance J. Herdegen, "The Lieutenant Who Arrested a General," Gettysburg Magazine, 4: 25-32.
94. John Busey and David Martin, Regimental Strengths and Losses at Gettysburg (Hightstown, New Jersey, 1986), 28.
95. Edmund L. Dana, Diary of Edmund L. Dana. Edmund L. Dana Papers, Wyoming Historical and Geological Society.

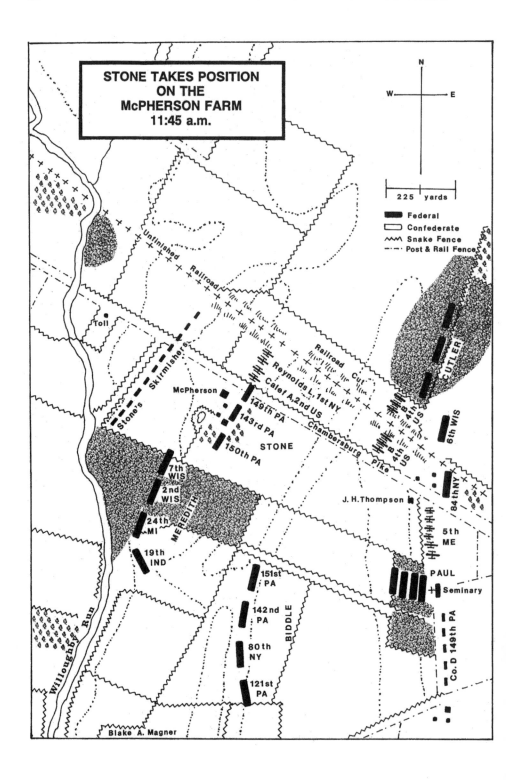

STONE TAKES POSITION
ON THE
McPHERSON FARM
11:45 a.m.

225 yards

Federal
Confederate
Snake Fence
Post & Rail Fence

Blake A. Magner

nies). The 143rd Pennsylvania (ten companies) was posted in the lane between the house and barn, and on his right, between the barn and the Chambersburg Pike he placed the 149th Pennsylvania (eight companies).[96] Stone's job, like that of Buford and Meredith before him, was to inflict as many casualties as possible and to delay the Rebel advance so that the town could be occupied in force by the Federal army. As it turned out, the heights south of town were chosen to occupy and defend instead. Stone reminded his men of the demise of Reynolds and encouraged them to avenge his death.[97] Such was the excitement upon entering the battle that the 150th neglected to load their muskets. Their commanders were reminded of this by the anxious cries of the enlisted as they moved forward into battle. Amid some subsequent merriment, their rifles were loaded on the run.[98]

A strong skirmish line was thrown out, one company from each regiment (Company A of the 143rd, Company K of the 149th, Company B of the 150th),[99] which made immediate contact with the Rebels. Additionally, Company E, 149th Pennsylvania, commanded by Captain Zarah McCullough, was ordered forward to the fence line beyond the Railroad Cut to warn of danger from that direction.[100] Captain George W. Jones, commanding Company B, 150th Pennsylvania, asked the regiment's commander Colonel Langhorne Wister, "How far shall I go?" "Go forward until you feel the enemy and engage him," was Wister's reply.[101] At a full run and without firing a shot, Stone's men drove the enemy skirmishers from behind a fence at the base of McPherson's Ridge. "These companies fought splendidly, and retarded the advance of the enemy greatly," remembered Colonel Wister.[102]

For the rest of the brigade back on the McPherson Farm, a modest shelter was offered by being positioned slightly behind the crest of the ridge. Unfortunately, the movement of the brigade as it took position drew the attention of Pegram's and McIntosh's Confederate artillery battalions on Herr Ridge. Their batteries, seeing

---

96. O.R., Vol. XXVII, pt. 1, p. 329, 332, 335.
97. *Raftsman's Journal*, Clearfield, PA., April 15, 1914. Copy GNMP.
98. Thomas Chamberlin, *History of the One Hundred and Fiftieth Pennsylvania*, 119.
99. Letter of Lieutenant Colonel Huidekoper to Colonel J. B. Bachelder, date unknown. *The Bachelder Papers*, 3 vols. (Morningside, 1994), 2: 953. Huidekoper in this letter claimed that it was Company G sent out as skirmishers.
100. O.R., Vol. XXVII, pt. 1, p. 329, 341.
101. John P. Nicholson, *Pennsylvania at Gettysburg*, 2: 746.
102. O.R., Vol. XXVII, pt. 1, p. 332.

Stone's colors moving behind the ridge, immediately began to inflict substantial damage on the prone Pennsylvania troops. Lieutenant Colonel Henry S. Huidekoper of the 150th Pennsylvania recalled how their movement had attracted the enemy's attention: "These dispositions had hardly been made, before Pegram's five batteries and Garnett and McIntosh's eight batteries on the west of Willoughby Run, and Carter's four batteries on Oak Hill on the north, opened fire, and, for more than an hour, these instruments of death poured shot and shell upon every seen or imagined position of our men, until hardly a regiment escaped loss, and none annoyance."[103] Stone walked along the line and encouraged every man to keep close to the ground.[104] Francis B. Jones of the 149th Pennsylvania recalled that, "while waiting, the tallest man of my Company, lying next to me, was curious to see what was going on, and raised himself on his elbows. At that instant, a solid shot cut his head off, turned his body over to the rear, and spattered blood over my clothes. The shot buried itself in the ground behind my feet."[105] He went on to say:

> . . . we saw a continuous shower of six inch shot come over the brow of the high ground and go on until they struck the ground in our rear and continued their onward rolling and bounding, cutting down men, horses and fences until they passed out of sight, while shells were also bursting all around and over us.[106]

John D. Musser of the 143rd Pennsylvania later described that

> while laying at the barn, a few shells came booming over our heads, making many of the unnicated [sic] dodge muchly and now and then a wounded 'skirmisher' was brought in from the front, and taken to the rear, all of which had a tendency to make us nervous, and uneasy.[107]

---

103. Henry S. Huidekoper, *A Short Story of the First Day's Fight at Gettysburg*, 20.
104. *Raftsman's Journal*, Clearfield, PA, April 15, 1914. Copy GNMP.
105. *Chronicles of Francis B. Jones*, Copy GNMP.
106. Ibid. There were no six-inch guns on the field so the solid shot Jones spoke of was probably from one of the Napoleans, three-inch rifles or ten pound parrot rifles posted on Herr Ridge.
107. Musser to D. Ribu, September 15, 1863. Musser Papers, USAMHI, Copy GNMP.

Perhaps out of nervous excitement, John S. Weber of Company F, 150th Pennsylvania, disregarded the relative safety of the prone position and stood up shouting, "Come, boys, choose your partners! The ball is about to open! Don't you hear the music?"[108] Others chose to use the time to refresh themselves. Simon Hubler of the 143rd Pennsylvania recalled, "At a farm house which stood near the barn there was a deep well from which the water was taken by means of a well sweep. The boys were making rather good use of this well, when an officer cut the rope allowing the bucket to fall to the bottom. His purpose was evidently to prevent the men from indulging too freely in the cold water in their overheated condition."[109] Ironically, around the same time, Captain George W. Jones of Company B, 150th Pennsylvania, sent William Rodearmal to fill canteens. This he gladly did but was not seen again until three days later. When he reappeared on July 4, "he presented himself before the captain on Cemetery Ridge with a large collection of freshly filled canteens, and with inimitable assurance said, 'Captain, here's the water. I knew you wanted good water, so I thought I'd go back to Germantown for it, but the provost guard stopped me in Baltimore.' True enough, he had started for home, but was arrested on the way and returned to the army under guard."[110]

In addition to the artillery, Rebel skirmishers kept up a hot fire from the fields west of the farm. "The air was full of bullets," remembered one Bucktail captain.[111] Jacob Yale of the 143rd Pennsylvania was standing near the McPherson barn when a bullet struck him above the eye killing him instantly. Because of their skirmishers out front, the men of the Bucktail brigade were forced to restrain themselves from firing. Simon Hubler remembered that, "we were not allowed to fire for fear of injuring our own troops, although the mini-balls were falling among us with uncomfortable frequency."[112] At one point the contest between Federal and Rebel skirmishers along Willoughby Run became so intense that Lieutenant Henry Chancellor of Company G, 150th Pennsylvania, requested permission to join the engagement with his company. He was granted his request but soon found that, because of the intensi-

108. Thomas Chamberlin, *History of the One Hundred and Fiftieth Pennsylvania*, 120.
109. Simon Hubler Account.
110. Thomas Chamberlin, *History of the One Hundred Fiftieth Pennsylvania*, 117.
111. *Chronicles of Francis B. Jones*, Copy GNMP.
112. Simon Hubler Account.

ty and accuracy of the rebel skirmishers, advancing his command to the stream in the swale below was simply impossible. He remained briefly in support, halfway between the barn and the run, before returning to the crest of McPherson's Ridge.[113] In his official report, Colonel Walton Dwight of the 149th Pennsylvania summed up the intensity of the skirmishing and the performance of his men by simply saying, "Loss, severe; conduct, excellent."[114]

It was about this time that a slightly framed, elderly civilian gentleman from the town of Gettysburg with a musket in hand approached the left flank of the 150th Pennsylvania. His age along with his black silk hat and blue swallowtail coat brought him instant attention from the men in the ranks. Approaching Major Chamberlin he asked, "Can I fight with your regiment?" Just then Colonel Wister approached and demanded, "Well, old man, what do you want?" "I want a chance to fight with your regiment," replied the man. "Can you shoot?" asked Wister. Proudly he smiled and answered, "Oh, yes," patting his pocket full of cartridges. "Certainly you can fight with us . . .," said Colonel Wister sending him to the woods on the left which offered the aging citizen more shelter from the elements and flying lead.[115] This man was 69-year-old John Burns, a resident of Gettysburg, whose patriotic spirit had compelled him to pick up a rifle and fight alongside his countrymen in defense of his hometown. For his efforts he would be badly wounded and left on the field. Surviving the battle, he would achieve some fame for his part in the fight. Later he was awarded a pension and was personally commended by Lincoln for his bravery.

Intense skirmishing with the advanced elements of Heth's Division continued throughout the early afternoon.[116] Sometime between 12:00 and 1:00 P.M., as Major General Robert E. Rodes's Confederate division began to arrive on the field, Lieutenant Colonel Thomas H. Carter's artillery battalion, which had preceded the infantry of that division, unlimbered on Oak Hill and began "a most destructive enfilade" of Stone's position on McPherson Ridge. Colonel Wister later recalled that, "Colonel Stone ordered a change to be made . . . as the range of the enemy's guns was so exact."[117]

113. John P. Nicholson, *Pennsylvania at Gettysburg*, 2: 752.
114. O.R., Vol. XXVII, pt. 1, p. 341.
115. Thomas Chamberlin, *History of the One Hundred and Fiftieth Pennsylvania*, 121-122.
116. William H. Wright to Mary E. Wright, July 7, 1863. Copy GNMP. "We was under the reb fire all the time."
117. O.R., Vol. XXVII, pt. 1, pp. 329, 332.

Dr. James Fulton, surgeon of the 143rd Pennsylvania, was horrified by the scene that confronted him upon his arrival at the McPherson house, which he had heard was being used as a hospital. "There was presented a sad spectacle. Spread over the floor the men of the battery [Calef's] lay, wounded and bleeding. There was no one to care for them. I looked around for my Orderly. He was nowhere to be seen. His duty was to carry the instruments, bandages and medicines. I had nothing to work with, consequently could do nothing without those things." Dr. Fulton made do with what he could find in the McPherson house and then returned to the Seminary looking for his orderly and equipment. While there he was ordered back to the town to work, which left the wounded lying at the McPherson Farm to the surgeons of the other regiments.[118]

Until the arrival of Stone, Lieutenant John H. Calef's Battery stood alone on the crest of McPherson's Ridge south of the pike. They had kept up a hot duel with Pegram and McIntosh on the opposite ridge as well as keeping Davis's skirmishers busy in the fields below them. Calef's gunners were surely relieved to see the approach of Stone's men who pushed forward and cleared the fields of Rebel skirmishers in their immediate front. By the time of Stone's arrival, some of the guns had already been silenced and the ground was covered with dead and wounded men and horses of the battery.[119] James Fulton, regimental surgeon of the 143rd Pennsylvania, recalled the scene: "As we went over the ridge to take position we saw a battery stationed on the summit just to the left of the turnpike. Many of the horses had been killed, the guns silenced, and the wounded had been taken into a small stone house to the left of the pike . . . ."[120]

Colonel Charles S. Wainwright, commanding First Corps artillery, had earlier observed Calef's predicament and sent Captain Gilbert H. Reynolds and his Battery L, 1st New York, forward out the Chambersburg Pike, to his support. Reynolds had just started out when Carter's 16 guns opened on them from Oak Hill, raking their right flank. Calef remembered the enfilade fire of Carter's guns on Oak Hill, ". . . the projectiles skipping along in a playful manner between my line of guns and their limbers."[121]

---

118. James Fulton, "Gettysburg Reminiscences," *National Tribune*, October 20, 1898. Copy GNMP. Fulton set to work at the Third Division hospital at St. Francis Xavier Catholic Church in Gettysburg.
119. Ibid.
120. Ibid.
121. John Calef, *Gettysburg Notes: The Opening Gun*, 50. Calef claimed that Pegram and McIntosh had 36 guns between them and Carter had 16.

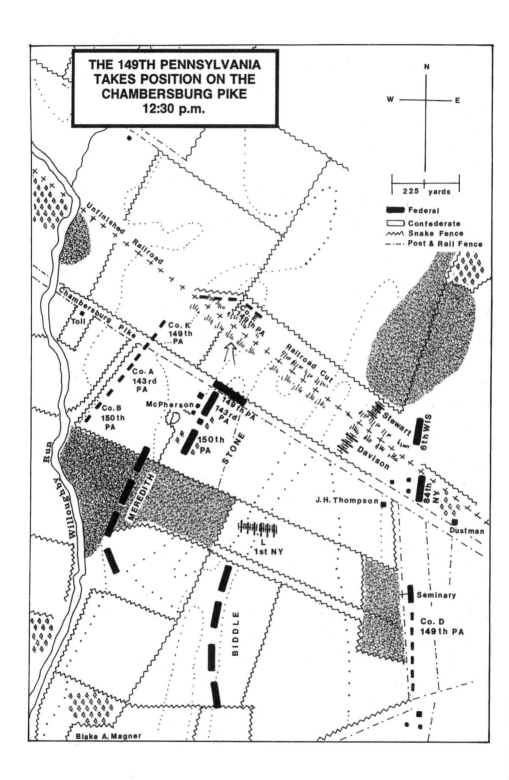

THE 149TH PENNSYLVANIA
TAKES POSITION ON THE
CHAMBERSBURG PIKE
12:30 p.m.

N
W — E

225 yards

Federal
Confederate
Snake Fence
Post & Rail Fence

Unfinished
Railroad

Chambersburg Pike
Toll

Co. E
149th PA
Co. K
149th
PA

Railroad Cut

Co. A
143rd
PA

McPherson
149th PA
143rd
PA

Stewart

6th WIS

Co. B
150th
PA

150th
PA

STONE

Davison

Run

MEREDITH

J. H. Thompson

84th
NY

Willoughby

Dustman

L
1st NY

BIDDLE

Seminary

Co. D
149th PA

Blake A. Magner

Cutler, who was also taking punishment from the guns posted on Oak Hill, moved his brigade to the rear, taking safety in the woods on Seminary Ridge. With supports on their right pulled out, Calef and Reynolds were forced to retire. "Ewell's artillery made the position untenable . . . ," Calef later said.[122] Calef's battery headed for the rear and did not stop until they had reached Gamble's cavalry who were guarding the Federal left. Reynolds's battery was now commanded by Lieutenant George Breck. Reynolds himself had been severely wounded in the face. Breck galloped south and placed his command on the crest of East McPherson's Ridge facing north with McPherson's Ridge shielding the battery from Pegram and McIntosh. Relative safety now established, the battery reopened on Carter.[123]

The withdrawal of the artillery had left Stone's brigade alone in an exposed position on the field, the same position that Doubleday afterward considered the "key-point of the 1st day's battle."[124] With the artillery support now gone, the Rebel batteries could concentrate on the troops left behind on the ridge. Colonel Dana remarked in his Official Report: "The attack upon our right became so severe that a partial change of front was necessary."[125] The brigade had been in position only a short time when this movement occurred. Captain John Irvin of the 149th Pennsylvania reported that, "We remained in this position for a period of fifteen or twenty minutes, when our regiment was ordered to take a position on a road leading from the town . . . ."[126] Stone ordered the 149th Pennsylvania to change fronts to the north and to take position on the Chambersburg Pike so that his line now fronted two directions. This they did in good order while shells screamed in and burst among them killing and wounding many in the brigade. Some cover and concealment from Carter's guns was found in a shallow ditch running along the south side of the pike in which the men of the 149th huddled. Unfortunately, this offered them little protection from the eastward firing Rebel guns on Herr Ridge.[127]

---

122. Ibid.
123. O.R., Vol. XXVII, pt. 1, p. 356; Doubleday, *Chancellorsville and Gettysburg*, 135; D. Scott Hartwig, "The Defense of McPherson's Ridge," *Gettysburg Magazine* (Morningside Press, July 1989), 1: 19.
124. Doubleday, *Chancellorsville and Gettysburg*, 139-140.
125. O.R., Vol. XXVII, pt. 1, pp. 329, 345.
126. Ibid., 345.
127. The ditch south of the pike may have been caused by water runoff resulting from the macadamized pike. The pike was a toll road that had been paved with crushed stone. This required that the surface be built up to accommodate the stone. As a result, the sides of the pike were slightly crowned and therefore fell off into slight depressions on either side. The worm fence that ran along the northern edge of the pike was in all likelihood torn down earlier in the day by Calef and Cutler.

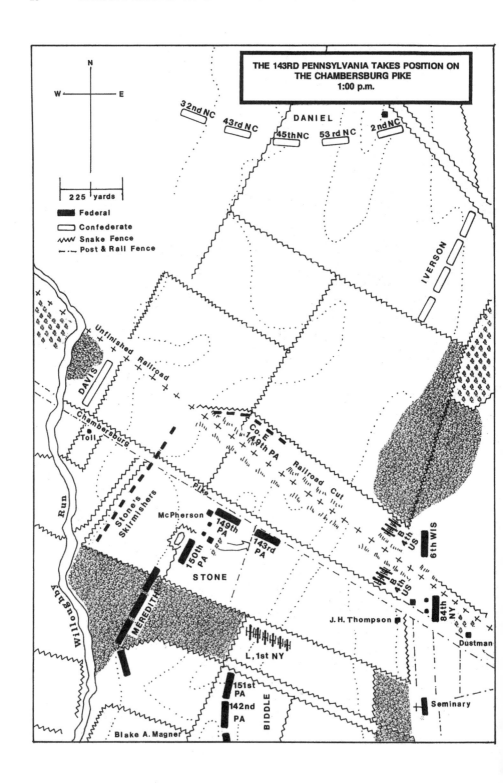

THE 143RD PENNSYLVANIA TAKES POSITION ON
THE CHAMBERSBURG PIKE
1:00 p.m.

Before long Stone could see a heavy force of the enemy forming for attack in the fields to the north. He ordered up Dana's 143rd Pennsylvania and placed them on the right flank of the 149th, thus extending his line along the Chambersburg Pike from near the crest of McPherson's Ridge to the crest of East McPherson's Ridge. Avery Harris of the 143rd Pennsylvania remembered: "It was here that we gained our baptism of fire."[128] Company E, 149th Pennsylvania, was sent across the pike as skirmishers where they mingled among the dead and wounded from the morning's fight.[129] The 150th Pennsylvania remained in their original position but lengthened their line to fill the space left by the 143rd Pennsylvania.[130] John Shafer of Company I, 143rd Pennsylvania, took the opportunity offered by his regiment's movement to invade the cellar of the McPherson house where he found a crock of sour milk. While enjoying the treat with his comrades, a shell passed through the roof of the nearby wagonshed startling them back to their senses. Shafer, suddenly aware of their predicament remarked, "We had better hurry up because the damn fools have our range, and somebody might get hurt." With renewed vigor the men returned to their commands.[131]

Rebel artillery also fell among the men of the 149th Pennsylvania. Company B's James Clark recalled that, "There was a shell bursted in our Co. It killed 3 dead and wounded 5 more, 2 of them mortuly [sic]." Captain Jones of Company G witnessed the same event: "A shell exploded in the midst of Company B of our regiment, on my immediate right, killing and wounding seven men."[132] Amid the confusion Colonel Dwight attempted to maintain control of the regiment. His courage would later be criticized by his subordinates as being induced by whiskey.[133]

By 1:00 P.M., about the time Stone changed front with the 149th Pennsylvania, Major General Robert E. Rodes's division was forming in the fields near Oak Hill. These were the troops that Stone had observed assembling north of his position. Despite being hidden behind the crest of McPherson's Ridge, the observant Rebel gunners on Herr Ridge had seen Stone's change of front and were making

128. Avery Harris Journal.
129. O.R., Vol. XXVII, pt. 1, p. 345.
130. O.R., Vol. XXVII, pt. 1, pp. 329, 330, 335.
131. Simon Hubler Account.
132. Richard Matthews, *The 149th Pennsylvania*, 82-83.
133. Ibid. Matthews's comments are without citation.

life difficult for the Pennsylvanians. Hugging the soil of their native state offered no escape from the sheer volume of ordnance being lobbed over the crest and into the suspected Federal position. By way of deceiving the Rebels into believing he had again changed front Dwight sent the colors of the 149th Pennsylvania, the center regiment which had been taking the most punishment, forward approximately 20 yards to the left front of the regiment. The ploy was effective. The Rebel gunners soon concentrated their fire on the brave color guard of the 149th who desperately searched for protection. They eventually found some behind a fence rail breastwork left behind earlier by Buford or Hall in the field north of the pike.[134] Here they hunkered down against a tornado of Rebel fire.

Wadsworth, who was keenly aware of his troops' situation on the ridge, sent to Colonel Wainwright a request for artillery support. Despite the overwhelming firepower coming to bear on McPherson's Ridge, he ordered up a section of Reynolds's battery (Battery L, 1st New York) under Lieutenant Benjamin Wilbur and posted them in the interval between Herbst Woods and the left of the 150th Pennsylvania. Here the McPherson buildings afforded the section some cover from the guns on Oak Hill. This enabled them to concentrate on the threat from the west. Wilbur remained here only a short time when his support troops (Meredith) began to fall back. The remainder of Reynolds's battery was posted in Wilbur's rear and was briefly engaged with Carter's guns on Oak Hill. After an abbreviated engagement with Carter, they noticed Rebel troops massing on Herr Ridge and changed direction to concentrate their fire upon them.[135]

---

134. John M. Bassler, *The Color Episode of the One Hundred Forty-Ninth Pennsylvania Volunteers in the First Day's Fight at Gettysburg*. Lebanon County Historical Society, 1907. Copy GNMP. William R. Ramsey to John H. Bassler, May 5, 1907. Bassler – Ramsey Collection, USAMHI, Copy GNMP. Harry W. Pfanz, *The Regiment Saved, Colors Lost*. By Valor and Arms 3 #2 (1977), 36-41. Copy GNMP. In 1884, Ramsey visited Gettysburg and measured off distances to various landmarks on the McPherson Farm including the position of the 149th's colors. He placed them, in relation to the Chambersburg Pike, approximately 32 paces west of the west façade of the McPherson barn and 54 paces north of the Chambersburg Pike. This makes the approximate position of the colors just north of where the Reynolds equestrian statue stands today. The advance of the colors clearly deceived the Rebel gunners into believing the regiment had moved forward but also resulted in delaying the Rebel infantry's advance because they believed that the Federals were in sufficient numbers to take the offensive.
135. O.R., Vol. XXVII, pt. 1, pp. 248, 356, 362. Lieutenant Breck reported that Wilbur's section only fired a few rounds before it retired with the supporting troops (Meredith).

Chapter 5

Daniel's North Carolinians Attack

"…a nearly continuous line of deployed battalions…"

Doubleday and Stone both reported that at about 1:30 P.M. they could see Rodes's Division emerge from the cover of the woods around Oak Hill and begin their advance upon the Federals posted on Oak Ridge. Wanting to come down quickly on the exposed angle of the Federal line, Rodes had neglected to throw out a proper skirmish line to probe the position. The Rebels advanced from the woods on Oak Hill and moved forward in total ignorance of what lay ahead. Stone recalled that "from my position I was enabled to trace their formation for at least 2 miles. It appeared to be a nearly continuous line of deployed battalions, with other battalions in mass or reserve."[136] As they advanced, the right flank of Brigadier General Alfred Iverson's brigade became exposed to the Pennsylvanians stationed along the Chambersburg Pike. Stone allowed his men to fire though the range was extreme. "We pored a most destructive fire upon their flanks," Stone later overzealously reported.[137] Simon Hubler of the 143rd Pennsylvania remembered: "[I] proceeded to put the powder from two cartridges into my gun, and rammed a ball down on the double charge. I then raised the sight to 900 yards and fired at some rebels whom I saw away off on the hill, probably a mile distant."[138] Though the damage that the 143rd and 149th Pennsylvania inflicted upon Iverson's North

---

136. O.R., Vol. XXVII, pt. 1, p. 330.
137. Ibid.
138. Simon Hubler Account.

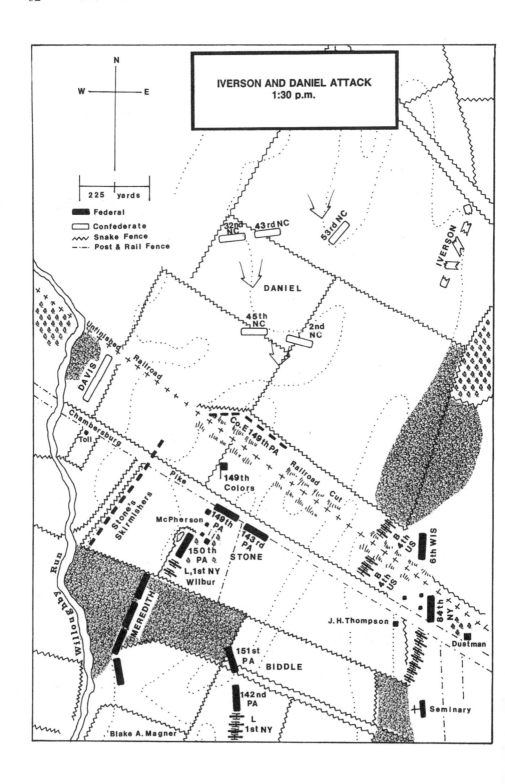

IVERSON AND DANIEL ATTACK
1:30 p.m.

Carolinians was probably modest, it certainly added to the surprise and confusion already present in the ranks of the Rebels. Panic ensued as Henry Baxter's men leapt up from behind a stone wall and unleashed the full force of the command upon the shocked North Carolinians caught in the open. The defeat of Iverson was nearly total, a high price to pay for foregoing an appropriate reconnaissance of the Federal position.[139]

By now, Captain James B. Stewart, commanding Battery B, 4th U.S. Artillery, had arrived on the field. Stewart's experienced eye scanned the field and quickly deduced the seriousness of the situation:

> I rode over to General Wadsworth and told him that the enemy was preparing to advance in his front, and to assist him I would place three guns on the pike and place the other three on the other side of the railroad cut. The general said he would be much obliged if I would do so. I had sent the bugler to Lieutenant Davison to bring up the battery. As soon as the battery arrived, I placed the three guns on the pike under Lieutenant Davison. I then placed the other three on the other side of the railroad cut about three hundred yards in advance of the left half echelon. My right half battery was under cover, being in a piece of woods.[140]

From this position the Federal gunners could see Rebel troops forming in the fields northwest of their position. In anticipation of what was soon to come, Davison ordered, "Load-canister-double!"[141]

Stone and Stewart did not have long to wait. Portions of Brigadier General Junius Daniel's Brigade, the 2nd North Carolina Battalion, and the 45th North Carolina Regiment numbering some 700 men, were approaching McPherson's Ridge from the northwest in two lines of battle.[142] Daniel advanced rapidly across the intervening fields halting only momentarily to cross the numerous

---

139. O.R., Vol. XXVII, pt. 1, pp. 249, 330.

140. James B. Stewart, *Battery B Fourth United States Artillery at Gettysburg*. Sketches of War History, Ohio MOLLUS, 4: 180-193.

141. Augustus C. Buell, "Gettysburg: Complete Analysis of the Official Records," *National Tribune*, June 12, 19, 1890.

142. The rest of the brigade had been detached to support Iverson's right rear. Stone may have observed Daniel while forming along Oak Hill. However, the rolling terrain covered with early July wheat may have hidden his approach until he came over the crest of McPherson's Ridge and was looking down on Stone's position at a distance of about 400 yards. Heavy June rains in the Gettysburg area had produced wheat that was chest high in many places.

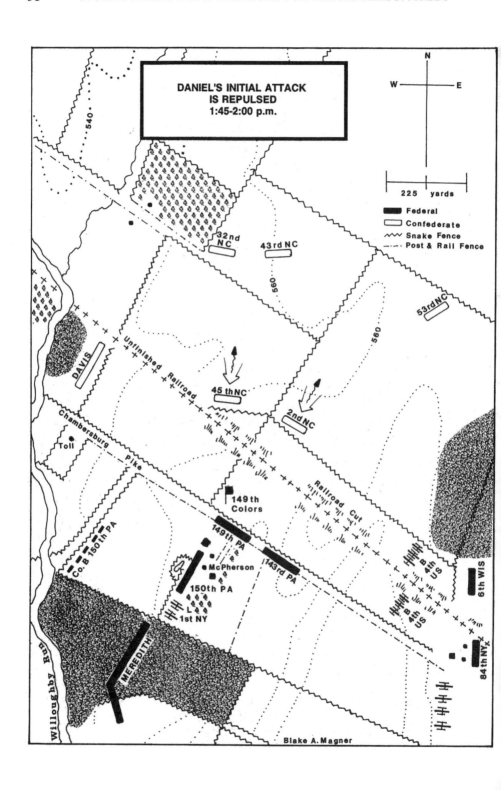

DANIEL'S INITIAL ATTACK
IS REPULSED
1:45-2:00 p.m.

N
W — E

225   yards

■ Federal
□ Confederate
〜〜 Snake Fence
—·—·— Post & Rail Fence

540

32nd
NC

43rd NC

560

53rd NC

560

DAVIS

Unfinished Railroad

45th NC

2nd NC

Chambersburg

Toll

Pike

Railroad Cut

149th
Colors

149th PA

Co. B 150th PA

143rd PA

McPherson

6th WIS

150th PA

4th US

L
1st NY

4th US

MEREDITH

84th NY

Willoughby Run

Blake A. Magner

fences transecting the Forney, Wills, and McPherson farms. William H. Wright of Company I, 149th Pennsylvania, recorded that "the Rebs drove our skirmishers in."[143] In all likelihood it was the skirmishers of Company E, 149th Pennsylvania, who were compelled to retire. They were on the brigade's right and therefore subject to the most intense pressure from Daniel. Evidence suggests that the skirmishers along Willoughby Run may have remained until later in the day when attacked by Brockenbrough. Thomas Chamberlin reported that they eventually retired and not finding the 150th Pennsylvania where they left them, fought in Herbst Woods and ultimately retired with the Iron Brigade.

Within moments of the skirmishers being driven in, Daniel appeared on the crest of the ridge above Stone. "First, we could see the tips of their color staffs coming up over the ridge, then the points of their bayonets, and then the Johnnies themselves," wrote a veteran of Battery B.[144] Moments later, as the Rebels descended a small rise and began to climb the rail fences that paralleled the north side of the Railroad Cut, a sheet of flame exploded in their faces. The slaughter was terrific, delivered as it was at such close range within 200 yards. Stewart's gunners took advantage of the stunned and stalled attackers a mere 300 yards distant[145] and opened upon their left flank with double canister, tearing great holes in the line and sweeping the Cut. "Ready! By piece! At will! Fire!" Davison commanded. "This was more than they could stand. They broke to the rear . . . ." Stewart later said.[146] In his official report, Daniel described the fire as he approached the Federal position as simply "murderous."[147]

While the Tarheels withdrew and regrouped, Stone, in anticipation of their return, ordered Lieutenant Colonel Walton Dwight's 149th Pennsylvania forward to occupy the unfinished Railroad Cut.[148] They did this in good order, their movements shielded by the

---

143. William H. Wright to Mary E. Wright, July 7, 1863. Copy GNMP. "My skirmishers were gradually driven in"; O.R., Vol. XXVII, Pt. 1, p. 342; Sanford Boyden to Ralph Gambell, March 15, 1906. Copy GNMP.
144. Augustus C. Buell, "Gettysburg: Complete Analysis of the Official Records," National Tribune, June 12, 19, 1890.
145 James B. Stewart, Battery B Fourth United States Artillery at Gettysburg. Sketches of War History, Ohio MOLLUS, 4: 180-193.
146. Ibid
147. O.R., Vol. XXVII, pt. 2, p. 567
148. The Railroad Cut was a result of the Gettysburg extension of the Pennsylvania Railroad. The Pennsylvania legislature temporarily halted work on the railroad in 1839 while they investigated claims of business impropriety but not before a series of "cuts" were made through Seminary and McPherson's Ridges. These cuts were steep and loose with rock. At the time of the battle they were also much narrower than they are today. As trains grew

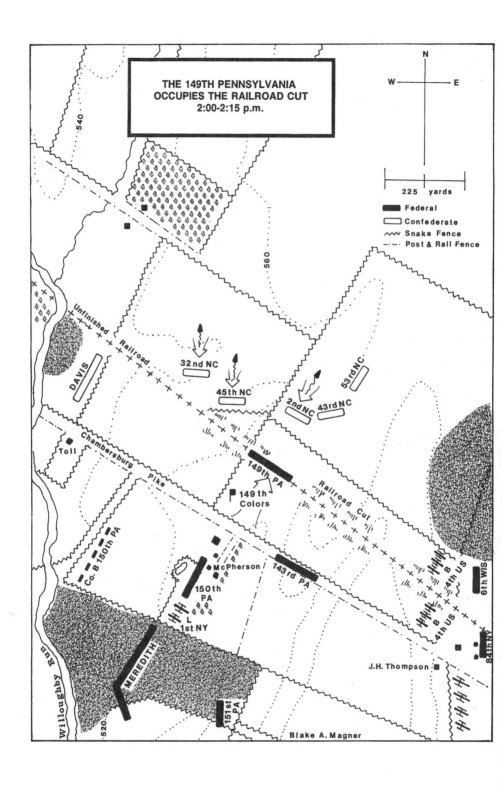

THE 149TH PENNSYLVANIA
OCCUPIES THE RAILROAD CUT
2:00-2:15 p.m.

225 yards

■ Federal
▢ Confederate
⌇⌇ Snake Fence
─·─· Post & Rail Fence

Blake A. Magner

tall grain and rising ground in their front.[149] Scrambling down into and then back up the far side of the steep cut was difficult in the loose, freshly excavated rock and soil. Men fell into rather than climbed into the ravine. Finally across, and now waiting for the Rebels in the cover afforded by the Railroad Cut, Dwight instructed his men to "take deliberate aim at the knees of the front rank of the enemy as he [comes] up."[150]

Stunned by the repulse of his initial assault, Daniel called up the remainder of his command, placing the 32nd North Carolina under the command of Colonel E. C. Brabble on the right of the 45th, and his remaining two regiments, the 43rd and 53rd North Carolina, in support of his left. Lieutenant Colonel W. G. Lewis of the 43rd North Carolina remembered:

> We were then ordered to move by the left flank to a position between the Second Battalion and Fifty-third Regiment, with orders to support either on the right or left, as necessity deemed. We remained in that position under a sharp cross-fire for some time, when we were ordered to join on to the left of the battalion and support it. The right of the regiment, in obeying that order, was exposed to a most severe fire in front and on flank, and lost very heavily.[151]

The 53rd North Carolina remained on the 43rd's left, facing Baxter and Paul in the woods to their front. With four of his com-

---

larger the cuts were subsequently widened. It was in these cuts that Davis and Cutler had so desperately fought earlier in the morning and where Stone and Daniel would come to grips later in the day. The reader should note that the Seminary Ridge railroad cut is the commonly accepted boundary between Seminary Ridge and Oak Ridge.

149. After the war, there were some conflicting reports regarding whether the field north of the pike was wheat or meadow and whether it was standing or newly cut. The author found that the preponderance of the evidence suggests that the fields north of the railroad cut were standing wheat while the area between the cut and the pike was a hayfield. Apparently, the intense morning action north of the pike had resulted in much of the crop being trampled, thus presenting a cut appearance.

150. O.R., Vol. XXVII, pt. 1, p. 342.

151. O.R., Vol. XXVII, pt. 2, p. 573. Nearing the woods on Oak Ridge, the 53rd North Carolina received fire on both flanks from Baxter and Stewart which forced a halt and temporary withdrawal to a slight rise in their rear. The 43rd North Carolina, upon joining the left of the 2nd North Carolina, received a galling fire from Stewart's Battery on their left and from the front right where the 143rd Pennsylvania was still posted along the Chambersburg Pike. They momentarily fell back until Brockenbrough and Scales were able to dislodge the Bucktails from the ridge. Having done so, it was the 43rd North Carolina, moving up the northern side of the cut, that eventually drove Stewart to limber up and retire. The 43rd's right would therefore have faced the 143rd Pennsylvania positioned about the Thompson house while the remainder of the regiment would have briefly fought the 6th Wisconsin in the Railroad Woods before they retreated to the town.

mands now advancing on the cut, Daniel moved off in another attempt to dislodge the Bucktails.[152]

As they came over the rise the North Carolinians caught their first glimpse of Dwight's repositioned colors and opened upon them. Stone's ploy worked and Daniel's fire was directed well left of the Pennsylvanians, the balls falling harmlessly among the chest high grass of the meadow. "[We] moved forward under a murderous fire of artillery in the most gallant manner to a fence, under cover of a slight eminence, and engaged the enemy at short range," Daniel later reported.[153] When they approached to within 22 paces of the unfinished Railroad Cut and halted to climb a fence, Dwight's men unleashed a "staggering volley" into them. Colonel Dwight would later report that "the effect on the enemy was terrible."[154] Surprised and confused, the Rebels again fell back to regroup.

They soon returned though, making a most desperate effort to carry the position and were delivered yet another helping of Pennsylvania hospitality in the form of another decimating volley. This time the Pennsylvanians could not be saved from galling casualties. Daniel's third advance nearly touched muzzles with the Pennsylvanians. In response to this, Dwight ordered a vigorous bayonet charge that broke them yet again, aided in part by Captain Stewart's guns that continued to pump canister into their left flank from their position astride the cut. Colonel Dana's 143rd Pennsylvania supported Dwight's position by keeping up a hot fire that managed to keep the 149th Pennsylvania from being flanked. "The One Hundred and forty-third Pennsylvania Volunteers during all this time had remained in their original position on the pike, but now poured in on the enemy, who were advancing on their front, a most vigorous fire . . . ."[155] John D. Musser of the 143rd remembered that "a few well directed volleys convinced them of the impropriety of moving in that direction and they fell back in less numbers, and in considerable confusion."[156] After falling back to the relative protection of the Railroad Cut, Dwight later said that "the enemy's dead and wounded [were] completely covering the ground in our front," a grim testament to the work that had been done there.[157]

152. O.R., Vol. XXVII, pt. 2, p. 567.
153. Ibid., 566.
154. O.R., Vol. XXVII, pt. 1, p. 342.
155. Ibid.
156. Musser to D. Ribu, September 15, 1863.
157. O.R., Vol. XXVII, pt. 1, 342.

The charge of the 149th Pennsylvania was not seen as heroic by all. Avery Harris of the 143rd Pennsylvania, sensitive to Stone's attachment to the 149th, related his sentiments in regard to the advance: "Stone is after a big chunk of glory for his tails and does not intend the 143rd shall have any of it."[158] There was probably some truth to this statement. A charge by *both* regiments would have produced a much more effective flank fire on Daniel's left and resulted in heavier Rebel losses.

It was around the time of the 149th Pennsylvania's charge on the cut that Howard arrived on McPherson's Ridge to discuss the disposition of First Corps with Doubleday. Howard informed Doubleday that he had deployed Schurz and Barlow's divisions north of town and that von Steinwehr was in reserve at the cemetery. Presumably they discussed the strength of the First Corps line and Doubleday's ability to hold it. Before he rode off to see to the Federal right, Howard told Doubleday to hold out as long as possible and then retire to the cemetery.[159]

Also at this point in the engagement, Stone was badly wounded in the right hip and was forced to turn over command of the brigade to Colonel Langhorne Wister of the 150th Pennsylvania. Stone was carried off the field to a makeshift hospital set up in the McPherson barn where he received care from his regimental surgeons. Sergeant John C. Kensill of Company F, 150th Pennsylvania, overheard a conversation between a messenger and Colonel Wister: "Roy Stone is badly wounded and you have to take command of the brigade."[160] The fact that Stone chose to be directly involved in the actions of the 149th Pennsylvania serves as evidence that despite his larger role as brigade commander his heart still belonged to the regiment.

Unfortunately for Dwight, the safety afforded by the Railroad Cut soon vanished as Brander's Battery (Letcher Artillery) of Pegram's Battalion dropped trail in the western end of the man-made ravine and enfiladed the position with canister, thus making it untenable.[161] McIntosh later wrote that "a fine opportunity was

158. Avery Harris Journal.
159. O.R., Vol. XXVII, pt. 1, pp. 702-703. Coddington, *The Gettysburg Campaign*, 282.
160. O.R., Vol. XXVII, pt. 1, p. 332; Matthews, *The 149th Pennsylvania*, 89; Letter of Sergeant John C. Kensill to H. Bassler, February 14, 1882. *The Bachelder Papers*, 3 vols. (Morningside, 1994), 2: 832.
161. David Martin, *Gettysburg July 1*, 243; John F. Krumwiede, "A July Afternoon on McPherson's Ridge," *The Gettysburg Magazine*, 21: 34. The exact location of the guns is unknown. However, a number of accounts state that from their location they were able to enfilade the entire cut. Because of the steep walled nature of the ravine, this

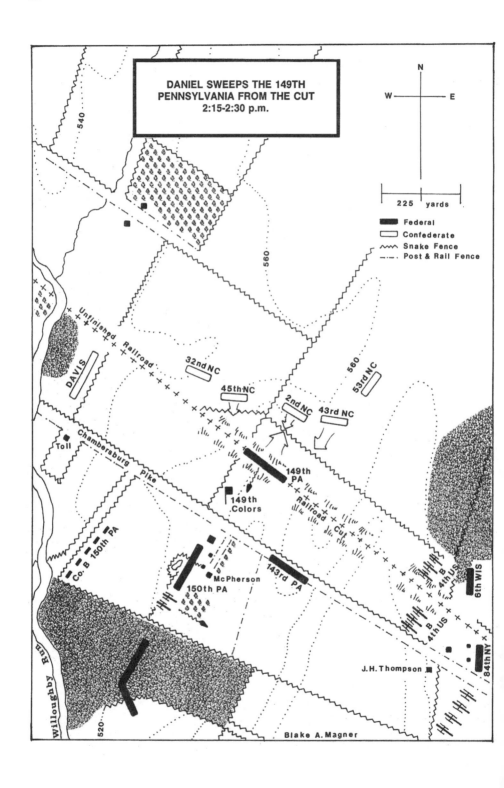

afforded at this time of enfilading a heavy column of the enemy's infantry, formed in the railroad cut and along a line of fence, which was employed to advantage by my batteries in connection with Major Pegram's, and the enemy, entirely discomfited, disappeared from the field."[162] With Brander's arrival, Dwight prudently ordered a retreat.

Trapped on the left by the high, steep walls of the Cut, Dwight's command suffered cruelly as they attempted to regain the safety of the pike, leaving many dead and wounded behind. Daniel seized the opportunity and "advanced at a charge, driving the enemy from the cut in confusion, killing and wounding many and taking some prisoners; also compelling their artillery to retire from the barn. At the Railroad Cut which had been partially concealed by the long grass growing around it, and which in consequence of the abruptness of the sides, was impassable, the advance was stopped."[163] John Bassler of Company C, 149th Pennsylvania, recalled the retreat in detail:

> It was easy enough, for the Colonel and the companies on the right where the cut was comparatively shallow, to get back, but the further to the left the deeper the cut, and the more difficult to cross. Some were shot while climbing up the steep side; others losing their hold slid back, some ran to the right to get out; and numbers on the left never got out except as prisoners. For the foe was upon them before they could clear it.[164]

Captain James A. Hopkins, of the 45th North Carolina, opposing the 149th Pennsylvania, said:

> We were ordered to charge, in which a very gallant one was made, driving the enemy back, but could not reap the benefit of our gallantry as we would have done had

---

would have required the guns to be set up in the cut itself and sighting directly down it to the east. In addition, the use of canister would have required that the guns be within a few hundred yards. This would place the location of the guns somewhere in the area of where Willoughby Run crosses the cut.

162. O.R., Vol. XXVII, pt. 2, p. 675.

163. O.R., Vol. XXVII, pt. 2, p. 567. These were Lieutenant Benjamin Wilbur's guns.

164. Letter of Capt. John H. Bassler to Colonel J. B. Bachelder, February 1882. *The Bachelder Papers*, 3 vols. (Morningside, 1994), 2: 830.

it not been for a deep railroad cut, in which about one fourth of the regiment went to the bottom. The remainder fell back some fifty paces. Those who were in the cut soon came out, bringing with them several squads of prisoners, some 20 or 30 in number. The line was then formed on the crest of a hill, where we retained our position under a heavy fire of grape, canister and musketry.[165]

Isaac B. Noecker recalled that "R. D. Spangler, as he was trying to get out, fell back into the cut again and broke his arm. He tried it again, however, and got out before the rebels had a chance to pick him up."[166] Francis B. Jones made it across the cut but had difficulty regaining the Chambersburg Pike:

While our regiment was about the middle of the field, I was struck by a bullet that passed through my leg, and at the same time, a fragment of a shell struck the same leg while it was in the air, fracturing the bone. As I attempted to make the next step, my leg would not support me, and I fell to the ground, while our troops went back to their rallying line. The rain of the bursting shells and bullets was so thick about me that the entire hayfield was mown down as if a scythe had cut it off.[167]

On the right, where the 143rd Pennsylvania was attempting to keep the 2nd and 45th North Carolina from flanking the 149th Pennsylvania, Josiah Wolf, of Company I, who had a problem with his musket, approached Corporal Simon Hubler. Perhaps because of nerves and inexperience, Wolf had rammed two charges into his Enfield and was afraid to fire the weapon. Hubler said, "All right, give it to me." Taking the musket and firing it, Hubler remembered that, "The recoil was terrific. I am of the opinion that he had five or six charges in, instead of two."[168] Lieutenant Colonel John Musser, also of the 143rd Pennsylvania, witnessed the 2nd North Carolina surging toward the cut and immediately ordered his men to deliver

165. O.R., Vol. XXVII, pt. 2, p. 574.
166. Isaac B. Noecker letter to the Lebanon *Courier*.
167. Francis B. Jones, *Chronicles of Francis B. Jones*.
168. Simon Hubler Account.

a flank fire to retard the advance. According to Musser, this fire "checked their impetuosity, and sent them back in 'Double Quick Time' without regard to order and lossing [sic] heavily by the way."[169] Colonel Dana, aware of the 149th Pennsylvania's position out front and determined that none shall fall victim to friendly fire shouted, "Steady now my men, every one of you pick your man."[170]

After Dwight had brought the remnant of his regiment back to the pike, the 32nd North Carolina, under orders from Daniel to "get a position where he could reach the flank of the enemy,"[171] surged into the western most Railroad Cut from which they could pour fire into the Federals. Witnessing this, Wister split his own 150th Regiment into two wings. The right wing (Companies A, F, and D) commanded by Lieutenant Colonel Henry S. Huidekoper changed front under a hot fire and went forward into position on the left of the badly battered 149th Pennsylvania. Captain John Bassler of Company C, 149th Pennsylvania, recalled: "I noticed to the left of our former position, the right of the 150th moving up to the post and rail fence, south of the pike, and opening upon our pursuers . . . ."[172] The left wing of the 150th Pennsylvania under Major Thomas Chamberlin remained in position facing west. The 150th's color-bearer Sergeant Peiffer received orders from Huidekoper to move forward toward the cut in the hopes of inspiring the troops. Bravely marching forward into a deadly hail of Rebel lead, Peiffer was quickly brought down along with the rest of the color guard. The advance of the 150th Pennsylvania was quickly curtailed by the approach of the 32nd North Carolina. Samuel P. Gilmore took the staff from Peiffer's grip and hurried them back to the safety of the regiment. The colors would eventually make it into the hands of Corporal Rodney Conner who was captured on the retreat through town along with the colors.[173]

Wister was keenly aware that to leave the 32nd North Carolina in the cut would result in the capture or destruction of the brigade and the loss of the position. Colonel Wister related that "the enemy had also, under face of a heavy fire from the One hundred and forty-

169. Musser to D. Ribu, December 10, 1863. Musser Papers, USAMHI, Copy GNMP.
170. Avery Harris Journal.
171. O.R., Vol. XXVII, pt. 2, p. 566.
172. Letter of Capt. John H. Bassler to Colonel J. B. Bachelder, February 1882. *The Bachelder Papers*, 3 vols. (Morningside, 1994), 2: 830.
173. Thomas Chamberlin, *History of the One Hundred and Fiftieth Pennsylvania*, 138.

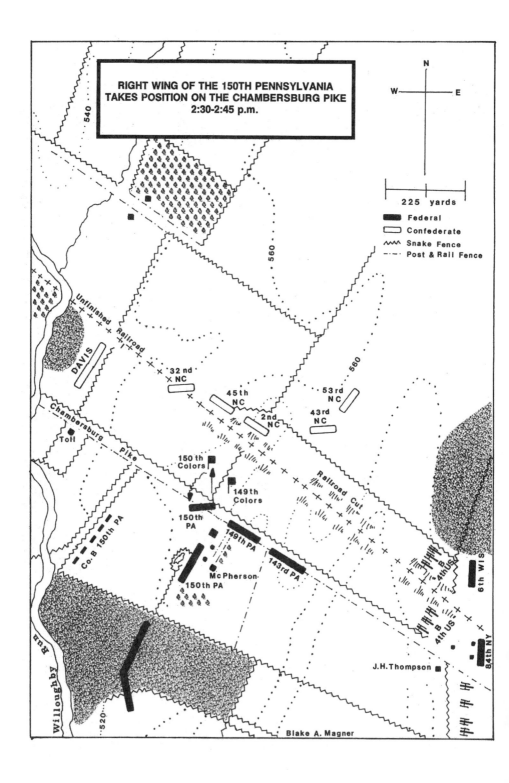

RIGHT WING OF THE 150TH PENNSYLVANIA
TAKES POSITION ON THE CHAMBERSBURG PIKE
2:30-2:45 p.m.

225 yards

Federal
Confederate
Snake Fence
Post & Rail Fence

Blake A. Magner

third, succeeded in occupying the railroad cut I had just vacated."[174] Without delay Wister called up Dwight's exhausted regiment along with that portion of the 150th Pennsylvania stationed along the pike and ordered them once again to countercharge the Cut and drive the Rebels from the ravine. This they did, although with galling casualties. John Bassler remembered that "this charge cost us dearer than the enemy."[175] Francis B. Jones, who had earlier been wounded twice in the leg and left on the field when the 149th Pennsylvania retired back to the pike, was elated to see his comrades return and press the Rebels back across the cut. In his chronicles, Jones remembered he heard two men of his company looking for him. Carried back to the pike by four men of his company, one who was wounded for his effort, Jones remembered witnessing Dwight's bravado as he led his men forward through the rain of fire.[176]

The pressure was too much and Daniel ordered his exhausted troops back to the crest of the ridge in order to regain some cover. "Seeing that it was impossible to advance this part of the line, and the ground afforded no cover, I ordered the 45th and the 2nd battalion to fall back some forty yards to the crest of a hill, which afforded some shelter."[177] From here he was able to keep up a heavy volume of fire on the Pennsylvanians.[178] It was as a result of this fire that many of the high-ranking officers in the brigade began to drop. Dwight received a serious thigh wound—Jones remembered seeing him limping and leaning on his sword for support while encouraging his men forward. Chamberlin was shot in the breast and shoulder and Huidekoper went down with a nasty wound in his right upper limb that would cost him the arm.[179] Wister, though part of his jaw and mouth had been torn away by a Rebel ball, continued to lead. Before long he was required to turn over command of the brigade to Colonel Edmund L. Dana of the 143rd Pennsylvania when the bleeding became too profuse.[180] The severe loss of officers

---

174. O.R., Vol. XXVII, pt. 1, p. 343.
175. Letter of Capt. John H. Bassler to Colonel J. B. Bachelder.
176. Francis B. Jones, *Chronicles of Francis B. Jones.*
177. O.R., Vol. XXVII, pt. 2, p. 567.
178. O.R., Vol. XXVII, pt. 2, p. 567.
179. O.R., Vol. XXVII, pt. 1, p. 333. The 24-year-old Huidekoper later received the Medal of Honor on May 27, 1905, for remaining on the field and directing troops after this grievous wound. He died November 9, 1918, at the age of 79 and is buried in Greendale Cemetery in Meadville, Pennsylvania. Along with Huidekoper, J. Monroe Reisinger of Company H, 150th Pennsylvania, also received the Medal of Honor for, "Specially Brave and Meritorious Conduct in the Face of the Enemy." Benjamin T. Arrington, *The Medal of Honor at Gettysburg* (Gettysburg, 1996), 5-7.
180. Ibid.

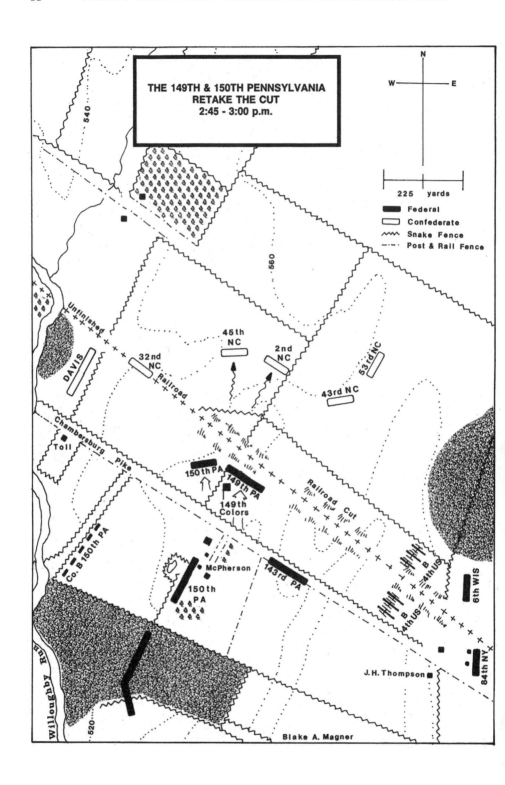

THE 149TH & 150TH PENNSYLVANIA
RETAKE THE CUT
2:45 - 3:00 p.m.

225   yards

Federal
Confederate
Snake Fence
Post & Rail Fence

540

560

45th
NC

2nd
NC

32nd
NC

53rd NC

Railroad

43rd NC

DAVIS

Chambersburg Pike

Toll

Unfinished

150th PA

149th PA

149th
Colors

Railroad Cut

Co. B 150th PA

McPherson

143rd PA

6th WIS

B
44th US

150th
PA

B
44th US

Willoughby Run

520

J. H. Thompson

84th NY

Blake A. Magner

in the 149th and 150th Pennsylvania now placed captains in charge of the regiments.

Sergeant William R. Ramsey, who had helped to bring Chamberlin into the lines, placed him on the floor of the McPherson house. He recalled that Chamberlin said, "Now boys, raise my head up, give me a drink of water and go out to your work."[181] In a newspaper article some 20 years after the battle, J. A. Walker of the 45th Georgia, who had been detailed to bury the dead on and around the McPherson Farm, recalled seeing Chamberlin sitting on the dining room table in the McPherson (Slentz) farmhouse:

On this table, sitting upright against the wall, was a Federal major, William or George [Thomas] Chamberlin, of the One Hundred Forty Eight, One Hundred Forty Ninth or One Hundred Fiftieth Pennsylvania Regiment, exact number forgotten. He signaled me to come to him, when he introduced himself and began a conversation. He had known several Georgians at school and inquired of them. Opening his shirt front he exposed to my view a ghastly wound through his breast, the ball, I think coming out his back, but he had no idea of giving up the ghost. I consoled him the best I could, but feeling inwardly that he would never see another day. His appetite showed no signs of an early dissolution, and dividing my biscuits with him bid him good-bye. I heard in 1865, when in Philadelphia, that he recovered from his terrible wound and rejoined his regiment. If this should reach his eye he will accept a handshake. Coupled with the mystery of his miraculous escape from the terrible wound is the equally miraculous digestion of those old biscuits.[182]

Despite having repulsed three attacks upon their position, the destructive fire laid down by Daniel's men was taking a heavy toll

---

181. Letter of Sergeant William R. Ramsey to Colonel J. B. Bachelder, April 16, 1883. *The Bachelder Papers*, 3 vols. (Morningside, 1994), 2: 949.

182. J. A. Walker, "Some Stirring Incidents," *Philadelphia Times*, Saturday, March 17, 188? In Gettysburg Newspaper Clippings, VI (Relating to the Battle), 13-14.

among the Bucktails and they were reaching the limits of what mortal men could endure. The 143rd Pennsylvania's Patrick DeLacy recalled the battle: "Bullets are whizzing over our heads and shells are tearing by us. One strikes me in the chest and rips my clothes to shreds." As luck would have it, the bullet struck DeLacy's cartridge box which absorbed the blow—"The cartridge box and the Lord saved me this time."[183] The intense fire was altogether too much for the badly mauled Pennsylvanians and they were again compelled to withdraw to the pike. By this time Rebel forces could be seen advancing from the west. "[T]he troops of Heth's and Pender's division in motion, descending rapidly towards Willoughby Run, regiment upon regiment, en echelon, followed by supporting columns, extending southward from the Chambersburg road as far as the eye could reach . . . ."[184] This eastward advance of the Rebels required the right of the 150th Pennsylvania to return to their previous position west of the McPherson barn facing Willoughby Run.[185] This was done " . . . with no undue excitement, and in thoroughly good order . . . ."[186] As luck would have it, it took Brockenbrough's Brigade time to get organized and their attack was slow in developing. Major Thomas Chamberlin of the 150th Pennsylvania recalled that "for some unexplained reason the strong force approaching from the west, whose front line was composed of Heth's division, moderated it's movements, as if awaiting developments on other portions of the field . . . ."[187]

Across the pike Daniel attempted in vain to illicit support from Davis's mauled and demoralized troops: ". . . I had sent an officer with a request that they would act in conjunction with me in my . . . advance, and with which request they had for some cause failed to comply."[188]

It could be said that the Bucktails' success thus far was due in part to having fought a single isolated brigade advancing from one direction. A.P. Hill, whose fresh troops were now formed and mov-

---

183. Patrick DeLacy, Capt. *DeLacy Describes Gettysburg Battle.*
184. John P. Nicholson, *Pennsylvania at Gettysburg*, 2: 755-756.
185. Letter of Sergeant William R. Ramsey to Colonel J. B. Bachelder, April 16, 1883. *The Bachelder Papers*, 3 vols. (Morningside, 1994), 2: 948.
186. John P. Nicholson, *Pennsylvania at Gettysburg*, 2: 756.
187. Ibid., 756. The advance of Brockenbrough's Brigade was halted as it approached the quarry at the base of McPherson's Ridge just north of Willoughby Run. The steep face of the quarry required Brockenbrough's regiment to shift north and south to avoid it.
188. O.R., Vol. XXVII, pt. 2, p. 567.

ing forward from Herr Ridge in an effort to overrun the Federals, would take special care to see that the Pennsylvanians' luck soon expired. There was simply no way that the Bucktails could withstand a concentrated assault from the north and west. The end was near and the Bucktails knew it.

Chapter 6

COLLAPSE OF THE SECOND BRIGADE

"It became necessary to retreat."

AROUND 3:00 P.M., Colonel Edmund Dana's situation became intolerable. Commenting on the confusion now pervasive in the ranks, Sergeant William R. Ramsey of Company F, 150th Pennsylvania, said, "[W]e were all mingled together, and it seemed to me that every man fought on his own hook . . . ."[189] Doubleday had recognized the imminent collapse of the line and sent word to Howard asking for reinforcements but had received no reply.[190] Daniel's Brigade was firmly positioned in and around the Railroad Cut and was delivering a massive volume of fire into the rapidly dwindling ranks of the Pennsylvanians. The brigades of Brigadier General Joseph R. Davis and Colonel J. M. Brockenbrough were slowly advancing up the western slope of McPherson's Ridge, firing as they came. To the north the brigades of Brigadier Generals Lysander Cutler, Henry Baxter, and Gabriel Paul could be seen retiring toward Gettysburg under heavy pressure. Rodes observed the First and Eleventh Corps begin to retire from his position on Oak Hill: "A portion of the force opposed to General Hill changed position so as to occupy the woods on the summit of the same ridge I occupied (I refer to the forest touching the railroad and extending along the summit of the ridge toward my position) . . . ."[191]

---

189. Letter of Sergeant William R. Ramsey to Colonel J. B. Bachelder, April 16, 1883. *The Bachelder Papers*, 3 vols. (Morningside, 1994), 2: 949.
190. Abner Doubleday, *Chancellorsville and Gettysburg*, 164.
191. O.R., Vol. XXVII, pt. 2, p. 552.

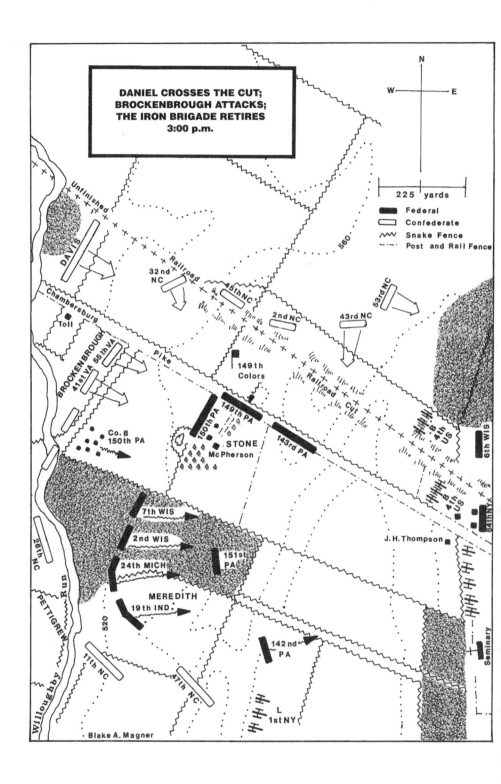

DANIEL CROSSES THE CUT;
BROCKENBROUGH ATTACKS;
THE IRON BRIGADE RETIRES
3:00 p.m.

225 yards

Federal
Confederate
Snake Fence
Post and Rail Fence

Blake A. Magner

South of the Bucktail's position, the brigades of Brigadier General Solomon Meredith and Colonel Chapman Biddle were in serious trouble as Pettigrew's North Carolinians began to flank them. Major Chamberlin of the 150th Pennsylvania recalled that:

> The attack on Biddle necessitated a readjustment of the line on his right, and Meredith recoiled from his advanced position in the woods to one vastly less advantageous about 200 yards further back. By this change, of which we were not immediately cognizant, the gap between the 150th and the Iron Brigade was immensely widened, and our left dangerously exposed.[192]

During the savage climax of the fighting here on the Federal left, Rowley, in an alcohol induced display of bravado, rode along the line waving his sword in a last feeble attempt to rally the troops. He had somehow become convinced that the loss of General Reynolds had elevated Doubleday to command of the left wing of the army and he to command of First Corps. During the withdrawal, Rowley himself added to the confusion by riding among the troops and chastising them as cowards. To their commanders he gave contradictory orders that only served to add to the confusion and delay the inevitable. His inebriation must have been so obvious that most of the men, officers included, continued on without pausing to listen to his orders. When it became clear that nothing else could be done on this portion of the field, Rowley and his staff rode off into the town, abandoning Stone's brigade. In his haste to retire and in his drunken state, he lost control of his horse and tumbled to the ground. His aides helped him back up and the party continued into Gettysburg.[193]

The withdrawal of Biddle and Meredith left a gap in the Federal line, which greatly increased the exposure of the 150th to flank attack. Dana, who was short on men and ammunition, would have risked capture or annihilation by attempting to stay on the ridge any longer. "His superior numbers enabled the enemy to extend his lines, so as to threaten both our flanks and rear," Dana reported.

192. Thomas Chamberlin, "Address at the Dedication of Monument, 150th Regiment Infantry," in John P. Nicholson, *Pennsylvania at Gettysburg*, 2 Vols. (Harrisburg, Pennsylvania: State Printer, 1904), 2: 745.
193. Lance Herdegen, "The Lieutenant Who Arrested a General," *Gettysburg Magazine*, 4: 25-32.

Caring for wounded in the McPherson house, Corporal Sanford N. Boyden of Company A, 149th Pennsylvania, remembered:

> [W]e tendered our services to the Major [Thomas Chamberlin] of the 150th Pa and he seemed glad to get a few recruits. Just then I stood within a few paces of him and looked back and saw a column of the enemy trying to cut us off from our support and retreat. I called the Major's attention to this and he said they were our support and not to fire on them as they were our men with the Stars and Stripes. I looked along their line and saw the Rebel flag over every regiment but the one in front and if he wanted to get out of there we had no time to lose and he then ordered us to retreat . . . .[194]

The Bucktails had delayed the Rebel advance on McPherson's Ridge as long as humanly possible. A decision to withdraw was required in order to save his command. According to Dana: "The heavy loss of enlisted men, made it necessary, in order to save the command from capture or entire destruction, to move to some point of support."[195] General Doubleday summed up the situation in his official report:

> The enemy, having been strongly re-enforced, advanced in large numbers, everywhere deploying in double and triple lines, overlapping our left for a third of a mile, pressing heavily upon our right, and overwhelming our center. General Howard had no reinforcements to send me. It became necessary to retreat. All my reserves had been thrown in, and the First Corps was now fighting in a single line.[196]

J. M. Brockenbrough's Brigade of Heth's Division was now steadily advancing eastward up the slope of McPherson's Ridge south of the Chambersburg Pike. Davis's Brigade had advanced on

---

194. Sanford N. Boyden to Ralph E. Gamble, March 15, 1906. Copy GNMP.
195. O.R., Vol. XXVII, pt. 1, pp. 335, 336.
196. O.R., Vol. XXVII, pt. 1, p. 250.

his left with its right resting on the Chambersburg Pike and its left supporting Daniel's 32nd North Carolina as they crossed the Railroad Cut and struck the flank of the 149th and 150th Pennsylvania. Davis's men would advance no further than the crest of McPherson's Ridge because, as President Jefferson Davis's nephew later reported, "The men, being much exhausted by the heat and severity of the engagement, were here rested, and about sunset were ordered to bivouac about 1 mile to the rear."[197] The Mississippians' contest with the brigades of Cutler and Stone had cost him dearly and destroyed the brigade's fighting effectiveness.

The impetus of Brockenbrough's advance carried him up and over the slope where he slammed into the remnant of the 150th Pennsylvania and the left of the 149th Pennsylvania, which had turned and taken position on the 150th's right.[198] "Here I saw the Virginians of Brockenbrough's Brigade . . . driving the enemy in hand-to-hand fighting out of the houses and barns of which they made forts," remembered Jaquelin Marshall Meredith, a chaplain in Heth's Division.[199] "The firing of the enemy, who was approaching in front of the corps, now became fearful," wrote Colonel Huidekoper. "The severe loss attending fighting at such odds soon compelled our men to give way." Exhausted and nearly out of ammunition, the 150th Pennsylvania changed front and started for the relative safety offered by the defensive position established at Seminary Ridge.[200] In their haste, the Bucktails were forced to leave a number of their wounded, including Colonels Stone and Dwight, to certain capture in the McPherson buildings.

The observations of Colonel Wister were similar to those of Huidekoper: "The enemy slowly closing up on our rear in large force, also working in rapidly on our flanks, owing to the withdrawal of the First and Second Divisions and the breaking away of the Eleventh Corps on our right flank, we had no other resort left than to retire in the direction of the town."[201] He went on to say:

197. O.R., Vol. XXVII, pt. 2, p. 649.
198. John P. Nicholson, *Pennsylvania at Gettysburg*, 2: 695.
199. Jaqueline Marshall Meredith, "The First Day at Gettysburg," *Richmond Times*, April 12, 1896. Copy Gettysburg Discussion Group Website.
200. O.R., Vol. XXVII, pt. 1, pp. 346, 347.
201. Ibid., 343.

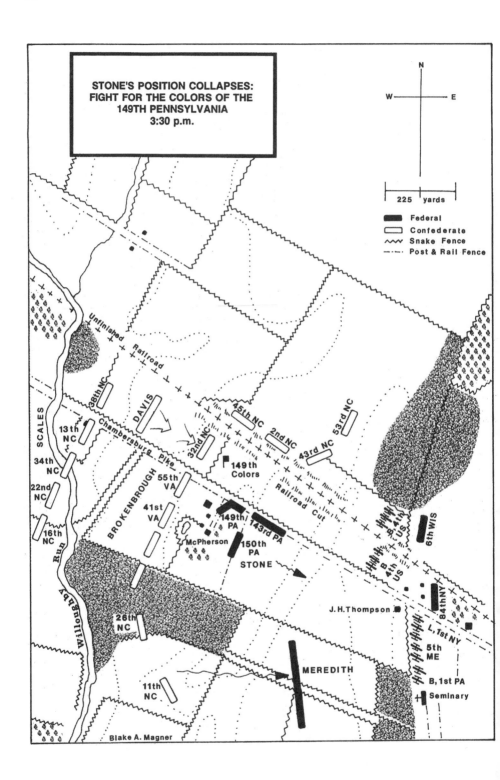

STONE'S POSITION COLLAPSES: FIGHT FOR THE COLORS OF THE 149TH PENNSYLVANIA 3:30 p.m.

The barn, which had been a protection in the earlier part of the engagement, as well as a convenient shelter for the wounded, now that the enemy had forced their way up to it, became a veritable trap for our own men. Those who were on the outside started toward the town, but a number had occupied the building, and were firing from every opening looking towards their assailants.[202]

One account by Sanford N. Boyden of Company A, 149th Pennsylvania, described the confusion that accompanied the order to withdrawal when he said, "I call it a stampede as it was every man for himself."[203]

Forgotten in the confusion surrounding the withdrawal, the color guard of the 149th Pennsylvania, until now positioned about two hundred feet in front of the brigade line, was left to their fate. The men of the regiment called out to them encouraging them to come into the line before they withdrew. Without orders however, Sergeant Henry Brehm refused to abandon his position. Brehm was unaware that few men still existed that could give such an order. Perhaps suspecting that they had been forsaken, Brehm sent Corporal Fred Hoffman back to get revised orders. Arriving at the last know position of the regiment, Hoffman found that all but the most desperately wounded had already retired. Glancing back to the position of the color guard, Hoffman saw Rebels approaching his comrades. Knowing that his return would mean capture or death he joined the ranks of his retreating comrades leaving Brehm to his judgment. Unfortunately, Dwight realized the color guard's predicament too late to do anything about it. To attempt to recover the flags would have meant destruction of his command. He later said, "I saved the regiment but lost the colors."[204] After the battle some claimed that Dwight's inattention to the colors may have been inspired by alcohol intoxication, though this was never proven. (Having lost their flag, the men of the regiment were obligated to invest in the purchase of a new one.[205])

---

202. John P. Nicholson, *Pennsylvania at Gettysburg*, 758.
203. Sanford N. Boyden to Ralph E. Gamble, March 15, 1906. Copy GNMP.
204. O.R., Vol. XXVII, pt. 1, p. 342.
205. Sanford N. Boyden to Ralph E. Gamble, March 15, 1906. Copy GNMP. Boyden claims to have had two dollars invested in the new flag.

A few men from Davis's 42nd Mississippi had been stealthy enough to approach the color guard hidden behind a post and rail breastwork. Leaping over the breastwork, the men of the 42nd Mississippi lunged for the flags and certain glory. Startled, the color guard rose in defense of the flags and fierce hand-to-hand combat ensued. The colors changed hands a number of times as attacker and defender punched, kicked, clubbed, and finally shot each other viciously in an effort to retain and capture the coveted prizes. The 149th Pennsylvania's Henry Spayd was eventually able to come up with the state colors and made an immediate dash for the rear. Regaining the pike, Spayd found Virginians swarming through the McPherson fields and buildings. He turned toward the possible safety of the Railroad Cut but was brought down by Rebel fire, his flag eventually falling into the hands of a victorious Mississippian. Meanwhile, Brehm, who had by this time retrieved the national colors, and the rest of the color guard, made for Seminary Ridge. They dashed through the advancing Rebels, surely taking many by surprise, having approached them from their rear, and continued on until they too were either killed or wounded. John Bassler, severely wounded and lying in the southeast corner of the McPherson farmyard, witnessed Brehm's flight for life before the national colors fell into the hands of the 55th Virginia.[206] Bassler wrote in a post-war letter:

> Presently Sergt. Brehm, all alone, with long strides, and the colors at right shoulder shift, emerged on my very limited field of vision. This was some forty to fifty yards off in the direction of the pike and in the edge of the meadow. He was quickly out of sight. My heart beat quickly as I thought of the tremendous odds against the gallant Sergt. A few moments later, and a red-haired rebel approached on his way to the rear bearing aloft our beloved colors.[207]

Spayd himself may have recalled the episode best in an August 1881 letter to John B. Bachelder:

---

206. John H. Bassler, *The Color Episode of the One Hundred Forty-Nine Pennsylvania.*
207. John H. Bassler to John B. Bachelder, September 5, 1881. *The Bachelder Papers* (Morningside, 1994) 3 Vols., 2: 760.

Our regiment was lying in the turnpike at the time we were ordered to plant the colors in advance. We advanced, as near as I can tell now, about 200 ft. to 300 ft. Of course was in a northwest, or left oblique, direction, so that by the time we halted behind a rail heap, we were far enough to the left to allow the regiment to move forward with a regimental front, and pass us without touching us.

Soon after we had planted the colors on the rail heap and placed ourselves behind it, the rebel batteries began to open upon us, exploding shell after shell either directly in front of us or immediately behind us; one of these passed through the State flag making a ghastly rent almost through the center. While this was going on we could see in front of us, in a wheat field and distant about 200 yds or 300 yds, horses, as though they were the horses of vedettes, but soon we heard the command given when we learned that it was the advance line of their infantry and that the horses were the officers horses. The officers having dismounted and hid themselves in the wheat.

We spoke of returning to the regiment but the Color Bearer, sergeant Brehm, said we could not return without orders. We suspected that the regiment had changed position, but we were confident, and so expressed ourselves at the time, that they would not move far and leave us alone with the colors in such an exposed position.

We had no time to look behind us and ascertain the position or the movement of the regiment because we expected to be attacked by the enemy every minute. Our expectations were soon realized, for with a dash and a yell the strong skirmish line was upon us and when they saw that there was no line of battle they all rallied in front of our colors where a hand to hand struggle ensued, not because we were willing to stand against such odds, but because Franklin Lehman who carried the State flag was wounded and fell, his flag falling across the rail heap and into the hands of a rebel who was lying or rather sitting upon his knees. Lehman, I think, still kept hold of the flag and another rebel was leveling his musket to shoot him, but I anticipated him & getting my musket just high to shoot him in the abdomen region. He fell and did not shoot. Time was precious and I was a good deal annoyed at myself that I had not made myself ready to fire before they came upon, by cocking my gun.

After I had shot the one who was aiming at Lehman I paid my regards to the one who held the State flag. He had by this time sole possession and was dragging it across the rails when I turned my musket and threw it against him with such force that he was glad to relinquish his hold. I then grasped the flag and made for the place the regiment had lain when we left it. In order to facilitate my speed I tried to throw my haversack away and was unfortunate enough to throw haversack and canteen, a rash act for which I suffered for the next two days. Instead of finding the regiment in its old place I found rebels coming in that direction and soon I was shot through the right thigh, but I did not despair of reaching the regiment, hence changed my course with the intention of keeping on, the rebels meanwhile calling "Surrender you yankees." I took probably 5 leaps after I was shot when I fell, managing to fall upon the flag intending to tear it from the staff as I had read of some who had thus saved their colors, but before I had time to carry into execution this design, the rebels pulled the flag from under me rather unceremoniously, and my career for the time was ended for the bullets came thick and fast and I stuck close to the ground in order to avoid them, hence I did not see what became of the other flag nor the one I had nor of any of the color guards.

After the firing had ceased I crept behind a small apple tree on the side of the turnpike. This tree was still standing when I visited the field in August 1880. It is nearly directly opposite the barn.[208]

---

208. H. H. Spayd to John B. Bachelder, August 1881. *The Bachelder Papers* (Morningside, 1994), 3 Vols., 2: 762-4.

Frank D. Price of the 42nd Mississippi offered a first-hand Rebel perspective of the affair:

While at rest the flags in front of us became an interesting topic of conversation. Among the many remarks made in regard to capturing them, fool-hardy was often used by the boys. I was lying very near Colonel M[iller]. Being somewhat rested, without permission or orders, I rose upon my feet, waved my hat, and made directly for the flags. When about halfway I discovered I was about to be reinforced by 2 or 3 men from the 42nd and if not mistaken 1 or 2 from the 2nd Miss. I did not know that Lieutenant R. of the 2nd, who hastened up and joined me in arms length of the flags. Poor fellow, in the very act of grasping the flag staff he fell, yes, fell, covered with glory fame and honor. Yes.

"Fame is there to tell who bleeds
And honor's eye on daring deeds."

But to return, when in a few feet of the rail pile, with 4 bright muskets with bayonets leveled at me I did not look back, but with a super human effort I cleared the points of the bayonets and with the P.A. flag staff in my left hand, and an Enfield rifle in the right, landed in a pile of 4 live Yankees. Now comes the tug of war in earnest. My herculean antagonist [Sergeant Brehm] bore one flag & all several yds. down the slope toward his line of battle: finally the staff was wrested from his grasp and away I fled back across the brow of the hill passing the rail pile, pressed hard by my heroic enemy. I became entangled in its long silken folds and fell! In an instant my pursuer is in five feet of me with the same bright bayonet at a charge. In a moment the bright musket lay upon the ground close by my side, he grasped the proud old flag and was making way with it across the ridge: as soon as I could recover myself, I pursued, when within about ten steps of him he stopped, dropped upon his knees, then slowly reclining, lay beside the flag, He was shot! I did not shoot him nor do I believe anyone knows who did, as there was constant firing from both sides. At this time, I noticed some of our men coming near him and knowing he was disabled I paid no more attention to the flag. As I believed they would carry it to my Co., which they did and awarded it to me.[209]

In a July 9, 1863, letter to the Lebanon *Courier*, Isaac B. Noecker of Company C, 149th Pennsylvania, described, "Thus the starry banners fell an easy prize in the hands of the rebels. The color sergeant and his guard here showed the highest qualities of the American soldier, namely, obedience."[210]

The color episode of the 149th Pennsylvania brings up two important questions. Was the advance of the colors away from Stone's position a tactically sound decision or an act born of fear? It is difficult to document a similar incident anywhere else during the Civil War. We are left to question what really motivated the change of position. Was it really to deceive the enemy into believing the regiment had advanced, or simply to draw fire away from an ineffectual commander? Secondly, why would the color guard have stayed on the exposed ridge during and after the numerous charges and retreats past their position? Surely they were aware of the impending crisis. Seeing the rest of the brigade begin to depart, would it not have been prudent to save the colors to fight another day? Leaving the colors in that exposed position was of no benefit after Daniel had discovered it was a ruse during his second advance to the Railroad Cut. Again we are left to ponder whether this was an act of blind obedience or foolishness. In his 1907 analysis of the color incident, Captain John Bassler derides Dwight for his order to advance the colors and states that "Col. Dwight was drunk during the fight . . .," inferring that this played a role in his decision:[211]

It would stamp him as a man lacking common sense. To plant the colors 20 paces on the left flank of the regiment with an overlapping brigade of the enemy approaching

---

209. Letter of Frank D. Price to Colonel Bond, January 27, 1878. *The Bachelder Papers* (Morningside, 1994), 3 Vols., 2: 525-6.
210. Isaac B. Noecker to the Lebanon *Courier*, July 9, 1863. Copy GNMP.
211. John H. Bassler, *The Color Episode of the One Hundred Forty-Ninth Pennsylvania*.

in front, could have done NO POSSIBLE GOOD. It would have been a senseless and criminal exposure of the colors and the men in charge of them, who would have drawn the enemy's fire with a vengeance, and would all have been struck down in a few moments, with the color company too far away to supply fresh victims.

The condition the Colonel describes as a reason for not being able to save the colors—out there at the cut—did not exist until an hour later; that is, after both wings of the brigade were left unsupported. During the greater portion of the time there was nothing to prevent him from sending an order to Brehm to return to the regiment.

The Colonel's well worded official report, so carefully drawn to shield him from blame, and which passed current these many years, is a dismal failure when subjected to the light of the truth; and standing out distinct and prominent is the melancholy fact that it was whiskey which muddled his brain that is to blame for the loss of our flags.[212]

When the 149th Pennsylvania's colors fell, members of the 143rd Pennsylvania, still exchanging fire with the 2nd North Carolina along the Railroad Cut, began to wonder what would become of them. From their position they saw the men of the 149th and 150th Pennsylvania move through their rear on their way to Seminary Ridge. Lieutenant Colonel John Musser claims for the 143rd the honor of last to leave the field. Having seen the 149th and 150th Pennsylvania retreat through their rear, this was probably true. It is also true, however, that the 150th had been pressed hard and had lost their support when the Iron Brigade retired, thus forcing them to withdrawal. The 149th Pennsylvania had made numerous charges throughout the afternoon and had lost severely. Considering the pressure they were under and their dwindling ranks, it was only prudent that they too retire. If the 143rd was the

---

212. Ibid.

last to leave the field, it was because their position was not as exposed to the intense Rebel fire on the crest and their being stationed further east and therefore the last to be fully engaged by Brockenbrough.

Feeling as though they had been abandoned or perhaps that they had failed to receive an order to retire, Lieutenant Colonel John Musser wrote that, "While debating in my own mind the propriety of leaving our position without orders, they came from Colonel E.L. Dana 143 now commanding the brigade."[213] Finally released from the hard restraint that had held them in their exposed position, the men of the 143rd Pennsylvania gratefully started for the rear. The McPherson's Ridge position had collapsed.

Before he retired, Sergeant James Rutter of Company C, 143rd Pennsylvania, performed one last heroic deed. Earlier in the action the brave Captain George N. Reichard had been shot down in the field between the Railroad Cut and the pike. Well liked by the men in the company, they were not about to abandon him to the enemy. Lieutenant John C. Kropp called for volunteers to bring him in. Well liked or not however, few men felt compelled to venture forward into such a deadly fire. Unable to bear the thought of leaving Reichard to his fate, Jim Rutter jumped up and made for the captain. Upon reaching him, Rutter recalled that "the Minies sang like bees around our heads." Finding that he could walk, Rutter got Captain Reichard to his feet and started for the rear. "It seemed as if the Rebels had made a target of the captain and myself, and seconds were like hours . . . . " Having passed over what was left of the fence along the Chambersburg Pike and through their regiment, Rutter and Reichard made for the safety of the Seminary:

> After a few minutes, having gained a little hill, I thought all danger was past, but I was mistaken, for I got in between the fire of the rebel batteries and our own near the seminary. As I walked along with Reichard, a comrade of my company, George Tucker, walked beside me without his hat, the blood running down his face. I asked him where he was hit, but he would not answer and instead turned now and then and started toward the

---

213. Musser to D. Ribu, December 10, 1863.

rebels. I would call him back and tell him not to go that way, or he would be captured. Then he would turn and come back to me like a child. I soon saw that a bullet had parted his hair in the middle, and that his brain had been affected.[214]

Sergeant Rutter received the Medal of Honor for his efforts to save Captain Reichard. Reichard survived the battle and was promoted to lieutenant colonel on June 8, 1865. In his report to Colonel Dana on July 4, 1863, Lieutenant Colonel John Musser erroneously listed Reichard as "left on the field." Reichard had been left in a private residence in Gettysburg and Sergeant Rutter had spent the night in Evergreen Cemetery not finding the regiment until the morning of July 2. Presumably Musser had penned his report having not been aware of nor witnessed Rutter's epic.[215]

Another Bucktail, Captain John Bassler of Company C, 149th Pennsylvania, had been badly wounded and left on the field. Second Lieutenant Batdorf of the 149th Pennsylvania came to his rescue loading Bassler on his back and carrying him to safety. This was no easy task considering the distance of ground covered and constant zip of Rebel bullets. Having achieved relative safety back on Seminary Ridge, Batdorf joked with Bassler not to give him too much credit because his object in carrying him on his back was to shield himself from Rebel bullets.[216]

In "somewhat broken order"[217] the men of the 143rd Pennsylvania "retired halting and fighting"[218] in a futile effort to slow the Rebel advance. In doing so they noticed that Color Sergeant Benjamin Crippen had lagged behind the regiment and in a last great act of defiance was periodically turning and waving his fist in the face of the enemy. Having angered his pursuers by these gestures, he became a target of some importance and soon fell to a hail of Rebel bullets. Lieutenant General A.P. Hill, observing this

214. "Sergeant James Rutter: Gettysburg Hero," *Sunday Independent*, May 28, 1989. For this act, Rutter received the Medal of Honor on October 30, 1896. The Wilkes Barre native was 22-years-old on July 1, 1863. He died on January 8, 1908, at the age of 67. He is buried in Hollenbeck Cemetery in his home town. Tucker does not appear on the 143rd Pennsylvania's roster of wounded and killed.

215. Report of John Musser to Edmund L. Dana, July 4, 1863. Edmund L. Dana Papers, Wyoming Historical and Geological Society.

216. John Bassler, *Reminiscence of the First Day's Fight at Gettysburg*. Unpublished address, June, 1895.

217. Simon Hubler Account. Sanford N. Boyden to Ralph E. Gamble, March 15, 1906. Copy GNMP.

218. Edmund L. Dana diary entry of July 1, 1863. Edmund L. Dana Papers, Wyoming Historical and Geological Society.

episode, displayed much regret at the fall of the "gallant Yankee."[219] Company B's Corporal Owen Phillips, who had thus far escaped injury, rushed to Crippen's side in an effort to retrieve the state and blue regimental colors. Gripping both flags and his Enfield he made for the rear. Colonel Dana, observing Phillips's struggle to regain the regiment, questioned why he had not abandoned his musket. Phillips's reply was both simple and sensible: he was just more familiar with his rifle. Dana, highly impressed by his actions, relieved him of one of the flags and promoted him to sergeant.[220]

Brockenbrough and Davis, having reached the crest of the ridge and now occupying the area that the 149th and 150th Pennsylvania had recently vacated, halted their parched and fatigued troops for want of stamina and ammunition. It was here that the fresh Rebel troops of Brigadier General Alfred M. Scales's Brigade of Major General William Dorsey Pender's Division advanced through the re-forming Virginians. According to Scales:

The officers on this part of the line informed me that they were without ammunition, and would advance no farther. I immediately ordered my brigade to advance. We passed over them, up the ascent, crossed the ridge, and commenced the descent just opposite the theological seminary. Here the brigade encountered a most terrific fire of grape and shell on our flank, and grape and musketry in our front. Every discharge made sad havoc in our lines, but still we pressed on at a double-quick until we reached the bottom, a distance of about 75 yards from the ridge we had just crossed, and about the same distance from the college, in our front. Here I received a painful wound from a piece of shell, and was disabled. Our line was broken up, and now only a squad here and there

219. Musser to D. Ribu, December 10, 1863. There were really three "color incidents" in Stone's brigade that day, each of them claiming to be the focus of General Hill's comments. Sergeant Crippen is displayed waving his fist at the enemy on the 143rd's monument along the Chambersburg Pike just east of the McPherson barn, presumably in the area where he fell. William Ramsey of the 150th Pennsylvania in a letter to Captain J.H. Bassler stated that, "I think the 143d should have been permitted to enjoy the honor claimed, more particularly because they had, to a certain extent, proved the correctness of their assumption, by the permission granted them to commemorate the incident on their monument, by the Battlefield Com." Ramsey to Bassler, August 3, 1906. Bassler-Ramsey Collection, USAMHI, Copy GNMP.

220. Avery Harris, *Personal Reminiscences*. USAMHI. The 143rd was the only regiment in the brigade to retain both of its colors.

marked the place where regiments had rested. Every field officer of the brigade save one had been disabled, and the . . . list of casualties will attest sufficiently the terrible ordeal through which the brigade passed . . . .[221]

Scales's troops continued to advance until they reached the lowest portion of the space between the two ridges about 100 yards from the seminary. One of the Wisconsin troops positioned among the Federal artillery on Seminary Ridge remembered the scene as the Rebels approached:

[A]t the same moment, as if every lanyard was pulled by the same hand, this line of artillery opened, and Seminary Ridge blazed with a solid sheet of flame, and the missiles of death that swept its western slopes no human beings could endure. After a few moments the belching of the artillery, the blinding smoke shut out the sun and obstructed the view. We of the infantry fell into line between the artillery sections and assisted with our musketry, keeping up the fire until our pieces grew hot in our hands, and the darkness, as of night, had settled upon us.[222]

Lieutenant Davison, now grievously wounded and unable to stand unassisted, but still commanding the left half of Stewart's battery north of the pike, swung his guns around to face the southwest so as to rake Scales's entire line.[223] Colonel Wainwright described the scene:

[T]he rebs were coming steadily on down the ridge in front only some five hundred yards off, and all the guns were blazing away at them as lively as possible. In a little time I went to the right and front of Wilbur's section, one piece of which was on the Cashtown road. I there found Lieutenant Davison has thrown his half Battery

---

221. O.R., Vol. XXVII, pt. 2, p. 670.
222. Robert K. Beecham, *The Pivotal Battle of the Civil War* (Chicago, 1911), 78.
223. O.R., Vol. XXVII, pt. 1, p. 357. This movement exposed the battery to an enfilading fire by the Rebel troops that by this time were moving up the slope of Seminary Ridge toward the guns.

"B" around so as to get an oblique, almost enfilading fire on the rebel lines. His round shot, together with the canister poured in from all the other guns, was cutting great gaps in the front line of the enemy. But still they came on, the gaps being closed by regiments from the second line, and this again filled up by a third column which was coming over the hill. Never have I seen such a charge. Not a man seemed to falter. Lee may well be proud of his infantry.[224]

Ordinance Sergeant Mitchell, of Davison's section, shouted above the roar of the guns, "This is tough work, boys, but we are good for it." As fast as they could load, Davison's Napoleons belched forth explosions of double canister that at this range blew huge gaps in the Rebel line and briefly halted their advance. "[The Rebel infantry] had been forced to halt and lie down by the tornado of canister that we had given them . . . ."[225] Scales reported that "the brigade halted in some confusion to return this fire."[226] Lieutenant Colonel Dawes of the 6th Wisconsin recalled that the Rebels "came half way down this slope, wavered, began to fire, then to scatter and then to run, and how our men did yell, 'come on Johnny, come on.'"[227] The sheer havoc caused by these three guns and their crews proved forever that the midwestern men who manned the pieces were in fact "good for it."

One member of the 38th North Carolina who now faced Davison's guns recalled, "The regiment being on the flank, encountered a most terrific fire of grape and musketry in front. Every discharge made sad loss in our line, but the troops pressed on . . . ."[228] Despite growing casualties, Davison's section hung on. At one point it even seemed that they had been victorious:

For a few moments the entire Rebel force, clear down to the Fairfield Road, seemed to waiver, and we thought that maybe we could repulse them, single handed as we

224. Allen Nevins, *Diary of Battle*, 235-236.
225. Augustus C. Buell, "Gettysburg: Complete Analysis of the Official Records," *National Tribune*, June 12, 19, 1890.
226. Doubleday, *Chancellorsville and Gettysburg*, 148.
227. Rufus R. Dawes, *Service with the Sixth Wisconsin Volunteers* (Marietta, Ohio), 175.
228. David Martin, *Gettysburg July 1*, 403.

were. At any rate, about our fifth or sixth round after changing front made their first line south of the pike halt, and many of them sought cover behind trees in the field or ran back to the rail fence parallel to the pike at that point, from which they resumed their musketry. But this second line came steadily on, and as Davison had now succumbed to his wounds, Ord. Sgt. Mitchell took command of the left half battery.[229]

Lieutenant Colonel John Musser, now commanding the 143rd Pennsylvania, retired up Seminary Ridge in front of Davison's guns, but found the western slope of the ridge too hot with flying lead to remain. He ordered the regiment across the pike and through Battery B to the area of the Thompson house.[230] Sergeant Ramsey of the 150th Pennsylvania, who had also chosen this route, later remarked that, ". . . it was out of the frying pan and into the fire . . . ."[231] As they passed, Lieutenant James Davison's section became aware that the 143rd Pennsylvania was their last support on the field and that they were about to be overrun. Davison exclaimed, "My God, boys, save my guns!" Musser recalled the incident:

By this time the enemy had advanced on our right, to within fifty yards of one of our batteries stationed there, and the cry was "save our battery . . . ." We turned upon them like tigers regardless of danger, with a determination in the mind of every man, to save the battery or die in the effort, and our effort was crowned with success, some pulled the guns away, while others kept the enemy back. There was a perfect shower of shells, shot and musketry poured into us, from all sides cutting the hay down around us, bursting over our heads and plowing the earth up beneath us . . . .[232]

---

229. Augustus C. Buell, "Gettysburg: Complete Analysis of the Official Records," *National Tribune*, June 12, 19, 1890.

230. O.R., Vol. XXVII, pt. 1, p. 339. The house was owned by Thaddeus Stevens and rented to the Widow Thompson. Evidence suggests that the house may have served as General Lee's headquarters during the battle though there is also credible evidence to the contrary. For a more thorough examination of this topic see: Timothy H. Smith, *The Story of Lee's Headquarters*, (Gettysburg, 1995).

231. Letter of Sergeant William R. Ramsey to Colonel J. B. Bachelder, April 16, 1883. *The Bachelder Papers*, 3 vols. (Morningside, 1994), 2: 949.

232. John Musser, September 10, 1863. Musser Papers, USAMHI, Copy GNMP.

Some of the Bucktails quickly surrounded the guns and helped to work them in a last effort to slow the Rebel advance. Simon Hubler remembered that the "artillery men worked heroically." One of the tubes had grown so hot that it immediately discharged when the number three man removed his thumb from the vent.[233] Augustus Buell aptly summed up the scene around the Thompson house by saying:

> We were formed in a small field just west of Mrs. Thompson's dooryard, and our guns raked the road to the top of the low crest . . . At this moment Davison, bleeding from two desperate wounds, and so weak that one of the men had to hold him up on his feet (one ankle being totally shattered by a bullet), ordered us to form the half battery, action left, by wheeling the left gun as a pivot, so as to bring the half battery on a line with the Cashtown Pike, muzzles facing south, his object being to rake the front of the Rebel line closing in on us from that side. . . .
>
> [H]is change of front gave us a clean rake along the Rebel line for a whole brigade length, but it exposed us to the raking volleys of their infantry near the pike [38th North Carolina], who at that moment began to get up and again come on. Then for seven or eight minutes ensued probably the most desperate fight ever waged between artillery and infantry at close range without a particle of cover on either side. They gave us volley after volley in front and flank, and we gave them double canister as fast as we could load. The 6th Wisconsin and the 11th Pennsylvania men crawled up on the bank of the cut or behind the rail fence in rear of Stewart's caissons and joined their musketry to our canister, while from the north side of the cut flashed the chain-lightening of the Old Man's half-battery in one solid streak!
>
> . . . Davison [was] on foot among the guns, cheering the men, praising this one and that one, and ever an anon

---

233. Simon Hubler Account.

profanely exhorting us to "feed it to 'em, God Damn 'em; feed it to 'em!" The very guns became things of life—not implements, but comrades. Every man was doing the work of two or three. . . .

Up and down the line men reeling and falling; splinters flying from wheels and axles where bullets hit; in rear, horses tearing and plunging, mad with wounds or terror; drivers yelling, shells bursting, shot shrieking overhead, howling about our ears or throwing up great clouds of dust where they struck; the musketry crashing on three sides of us; bullets hissing, humming and whistling everywhere; cannon roaring; all crash on crash and peal on peal, smoke, dust, splinters, blood, wreck and carnage indescribable; but the brass guns of Old B still bellowed and not a man or boy flinched or faltered! Every man's shirt was soaked with sweat and many of them sopped with blood from wounds not severe enough to make such bulldogs "let go"—bareheaded, sleeves rolled up, faces blackened–oh! If such a picture could be spread on canvas to the life! Out in front of us are undulating field, filled almost as far as the eye could reach with a long, low gray line creeping toward us, fairly fringed with flame![234]

This was altogether too much for the battery to endure. By now Davison was down, having succumbed to his wounds and Sergeant Mitchell prudently, though without orders from Stewart, ordered the guns to limber to the rear.

Around this time, the right half of Stewart's battery, north of the pike, received orders from one of General Robinson's aides to "fall back to the town as rapidly as possible." Later Stewart remembered that "for the first time that day did I realize the horrors of what war meant. As I gave the command to limber to the rear, I could not bring my wounded with me, and the beseeching looks that these men gave me quite unnerved me, and I was sorry indeed to leave them to their fate."[235]

---

234. Augustus C. Buell, "Gettysburg: Complete Analysis of the Official Records," *National Tribune*, June 12, 19, 1890.
235. James B. Stewart, *Battery B*, 180-193.

Stewart fell back with his guns through the boulder strewn Railroad Cut where they were halted when the pintle hook on the third piece broke dropping its trail to the ground. With Rebels swarming through the woods all around them (probably the 43rd North Carolina) Stewart ordered the first two guns to set up along the pike in an attempt to save the disabled piece. "Halt that piece" came a cry from the woods as the Rebels moved forward to capture it. "Don't you see that the piece is halted?" came the incredulous response from a Federal cannoneer. With that, the first two guns came to life sending the Rebels scurrying for cover. Under a most severe fire, the men of the 43rd North Carolina advanced through the Railroad Woods to a position where they could fire down into the section. The two exchanged fire from as close as 60 yards until Stewart's men were finally able to get the gun off and retire quickly back through the town.[236]

Positioned along the crest of Seminary Ridge south of Davison was the remainder of the First Corps artillery. Two three-inch rifles of Battery L, 1st New York, were unlimbered on the Chambersburg Pike. South of them was Captain Greenleaf Stevens's 5th Maine Battery with six Napoleons. On Stevens's left was Captain James Cooper and his four three-inch rifles of Battery B, 1st Pennsylvania Light, and south of the Seminary were the remaining four three-inch rifles of Battery L, 1st New York. William Ramsey of the 150th Pennsylvania remembered one artillerist crying out, "Stand to your work Bucktails, don't let a skirmish line drive you!"[237] In front of this position "the enemy fell thick and fast."[238] The Federal line had lost form as it withdrew to the Seminary and Stevens had to take care in firing since Dana's men frequently came into his gunner's sights. One of Scales men approached a battery and placing his hand on one of the guns exclaimed, "This gun is mine!" The number four man of the piece, in defense of his gun, replied, "Damn you, take it then," yanking the lanyard and blowing the brave Rebel apart.[239] It was around these guns that First Sergeant Weidensaul of the 150th

---

236. Ibid. These Rebels probably belonged to the 43rd North Carolina which had advanced up the slope and into the woods on its summit.

237. Ramsey to Bassler, August 3, 1906. Bassler-Ramsey Collection, USAMHI, Copy GNMP.

238. Report of John Musser to Edmund L. Dana, July 4, 1863. Edmund L. Dana Papers, Wyoming Historical and Geological Society.

239. Ibid.

Pennsylvania was seen to reel and press his body as if in pain. Adjutant Ashurst asked him if he was wounded and he replied, "No, killed!"[240]

Colonel Dana was briefly able to rally the mob on the crest of Seminary Ridge. According to First Lieutenant Jacob F. Slagle of Company D, 149th Pennsylvania, "We stayed there [on Seminary Ridge] about fifteen minutes . . . ."[241] The ammunition train was just beyond the crest and fresh ammunition may have been quickly distributed among the men before the wounded Lieutenant Colonel Huidekoper sent it to the rear.[242] Lieutenant Colonel Rufus Dawes, of the 6th Wisconsin, watched the action from the woods on Oak Ridge just north of the cut:

Along the Seminary Ridge, flat upon their bellies, lay mixed up together in one line of battle the Iron Brigade and Roy Stone's "Bucktails." For a mile up and down the open fields before us the splendid lines of the veterans of the Army of Northern Virginia swept down upon us. Their bearing was magnificent. They maintained their alignments with great precision. In many cases the colors of the regiments were advanced several paces in front of the line.[243]

John Musser kept the men of the 143rd Pennsylvania to their work firing into the advancing Rebels. He later described the situation in front of the Thompson house:

It was near a house on the Chambersburg Road, we had to cross the road in front, and endure heavy cannonading from a Rebel battery with no small peppering of minies and canister, but the resolve, was in the heart of every man, to stand by and save the [Davison] battery from the advancing Rebels, who were now seen coming in force on the right of the road, briskly loading and firing as they came. The [Confederate] battery was thundering shell

240. Thomas Chamberlin, *History of the One Hundred and Fiftieth Pennsylvania*, 133.
241. Jacob F. Slagle letter, September 13, 1863. Copy GNMP.
242. Lieutenant Colonel Huidekoper to John B. Bachelder, date unknown. *The Bachelder Papers* (Morningside, 1994), 3 Vols., 2: 954.
243. Rufus R. Dawes, *Service with the Sixth Wisconsin Volunteers*, 175.

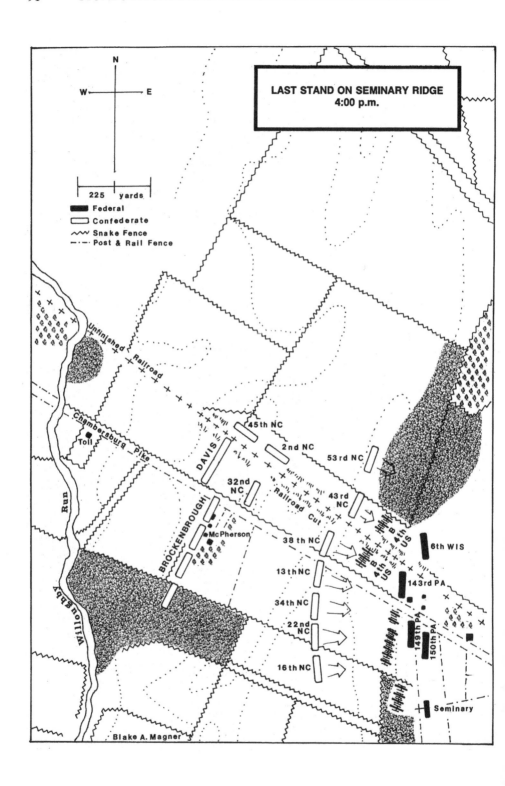

LAST STAND ON SEMINARY RIDGE
4:00 p.m.

225 yards

Federal
Confederate
Snake Fence
Post & Rail Fence

N
W — E

Unfinished Railroad

Chambersburg Pike

Toll

Run

DAVIS

BROCKENBROUGH

McPherson

Willoughby

45th NC

2nd NC

53rd NC

32nd NC

43rd NC

Railroad Cut

38th NC

13th NC

34th NC

22nd NC

16th NC

4th US

4th US

6th WIS

143rd PA

149th PA

150th PA

Seminary

Blake A. Magner

and shot among us, some bursting over our heads, others among the trees cutting them off, then as if not satisfied, bursting and scattering the pieces in every direction, killing and wounding as they went. Others came plowing through under our feet lifting men up in the air to find when they came down their graves already open. Still the 143rd stood to the work at hand . . . .[244]

The casualty statistics of the 13th North Carolina, which advanced against the Bucktails on Seminary Ridge, attested to the terrific slaughter as they ascended the ridge. Only 30 of the 180 who had entered the fight would crest Seminary Ridge unscathed.[245]

By 4:00 P.M., General Scales had reformed his battered Rebel command and was again advancing. The Railroad Woods had become uninhabitable on Dana's right. Daniel's North Carolinians and Perrin's South Carolinians had outflanked Meredith and Biddle south of the Seminary forcing Dana to retreat. The Bucktails had done all they could. All the bravery in the world could not change the mathematics of the situation—the position was untenable and it was time to get out. Colonel Dwight, when referring to the fighting on the brigade's right, complimented Dana in his official report by saying that "[he] did most gallant work on the retreat from McPherson's barn to the seminary, he protecting the flank resting on the railroad cut against great odds by the hardest fighting."[246]

During Perrin's advance toward Seminary Ridge, his right became engaged with Captain James Glenn's Company D, 149th Pennsylvania, which until that time had been acting as headquarters guard. From his position along the crest of the ridge between the Seminary and the Schumacher house, Glenn's 60 rifles "opened a fire sufficient to induce the enemy to halt, supposing that our forces had made a stand there."[247] Glenn recalled that they "opened fire and kept it up but the rebels moved slowly and steadily forwards, and it soon became evident that [they] could not hold the

---

244. John Musser, Musser Papers, USAMHI, Copy GNMP.
245. D. Scott Hartwig, "Never Have I Seen Such a Charge," in *High Water Mark: The Army of Northern Virginia in the Gettysburg Campaign, Programs of the Seventh Annual Gettysburg Seminar* (1999), 51
246. O.R., Vol. XXVII, pt. 1, p. 343.
247. John P. Nicholson, *Pennsylvania at Gettysburg*, 2: 747.

position. . . . It now became necessary to run to escape capture and our boys got off that hill in a hurry."[248] John W. Nesbit of Company D described their retreat: "We turned off to the right at the next street we came to and followed the crowd. . . . We followed this cross street up the hill until we were out of the town and then crossed a corn field and found the reserve division of the Eleventh Corps. We passed through their line over the hill, and completely worn out, dropped down on the grass and rested as best we could."[249]

Having gained the orchard around the Thompson house, the 38th North Carolina was able to fire into the flank of the remaining batteries posted along the ridge forcing them to retire in haste, some of them being drawn off by hand. Lieutenant Colonel Musser, who had sought some shelter in these trees, was surprised to find the atmosphere even more deadly here than in his previous position and ordered his men back across the pike. According to him "the balls and shells were as thick, if not thicker, on the right as on the left side."[250]

The artillery now nearly gone and surrounded on three sides, Dana finally ordered the Bucktails out: "On the withdrawal of the artillery, this command moved along the embankment toward and through the town, the last organized body of troops, I believe, to leave the field."[251] Musser recalled the hectic retreat through the town:

> A few minutes more and we would have been surround-ed, they were on both sides of us and as near the town as we were. A high artificial road [the railroad bed] lay across a wide meadow between the Peach Orchard and the town. It broke the enfilading fire on our right, we took the left side [south side], and moved rapidly to the town but in good order. There was no use in fighting any longer. The enemy had deployed and we were trapped. The town was before us, the enemy on either side, and behind us.[252]

248. John W. Nesbit, *General History of Company D, One Hundred Forty-Ninth Pennsylvania Volunteers* (Oakdale, 1908), 15-16.
249. Ibid., 16.
250. O.R., Vol. XXVII, pt. 1, p. 339.
251. Ibid., 336.
252. Musser to D. Ribu, December 10, 1863.

Musser felt a profound sense of loss as he left the field with what was left of the 143rd Pennsylvania: "We could only give a parting glance of sympathy to the wounded, and cast a sad look, as we left, upon the dead heroes who lay thick around us."[253]

253. Ibid.

Maj. Thomas Chamberlin
150th Regt., Pa. Vol. Inf.
(USAMHI)

LTC Henry S. Huidekoper
150th Regt., Pa. Vol. Inf.
(USAMHI)

Capt. John Bassler
Co. C, 149th Regt., Pa. Vol. Inf.
(USAMHI)

Sgt. Henry Brehm
Co. C, 149th Regt., Pa. Vol. Inf.
(USAMHI)

Corp. John Fridell
Co. C, 149th Regt., Pa. Vol. Inf.
(USAMHI)

Corp. Frank Lehman
Co. C, 149th Regt., Pa. Vol. Inf.
(USAMHI)

Corp. Henry Spayd
Co. C, 149th Regt., Pa. Vol. Inf.
(USAMHI)

Sgt. Maj. Patrick DeLacy
143rd Regt., Pa. Vol. Inf.
A Medal of Honor recipient
(USAMHI)

This Alan C. Redwood engraving shows Brockenbrough's troops advancing on the McPherson Farm from the west about 3:30 P.M., July 1, 1863. Note the heightened appearance of the McPherson barn. The ventilation embrasures are represented somewhat longer than they actually were. The lean-tos on the west side of the barn show the correct orientation of the board siding with the southern lean-tos' boards horizontal and the northern lean-to vertical.

This carving on the Pennsylvania Memorial at Gettysburg shows the troops of the 150th Pennsylvania facing west and confronting the attack of Brockenbrough. Harrison Granite Co., Contractor, New York; Samuel Murray, Sculptor, Philadelphia. (Author's Collection)

This engraving is from Thomas Chamberlin's *History of the One Hundred Fiftieth Regiment Pennsylvania Volunteers* (Philadelphia, 1905). It was Brockenbrough not Scales who first attacked from the west. It is apparent by the representation of the barn that the artist, Franz Lesshafft, was fairly accurate in his depiction of the building.

This view taken from a position south of the McPherson house looking east shows the condition of the Slentz's cornfield after the battle along with the grove-like appearance of Herbst Woods. Between the southern boundary of the cornfield and the northern boundary of Herbst Woods lies fencing knocked down during the battle. (Library of Congress)

Edward McPherson ca. 1876
(Gettysburg College)

View from McPherson's Ridge west toward the toll house along the Chambersburg Pike. Stone's skirmishers advanced past the toll house and into the low ground beyond along Willoughby Run where they engaged the Rebel skirmishers. (USAMHI)

View from McPherson's Ridge toward the Oak Ridge Railroad Cut. The left half of Stewart's Battery B, 4th U.S., under Davison was posted in front of the buildings on the right while the section under Stewart himself was posted in front of the fence in the grove of trees in the left background. The 38th North Carolina advanced with its left on the cut against Davison and the 143rd Pennsylvania positioned at the Thompson house while the 43rd North Carolina, north of the cut, moved upon Stewart's section and the 6th Wisconsin in the trees on Oak Ridge. (GNMP)

View looking west toward the McPherson Farm. The house and wagon shed are still standing indicating that the photo was taken prior to 1895. (Adams County Historical Society)

View from the Chamberburg Pike just north of the McPherson barn toward Seminary Ridge. The 149th and 143rd Pennsylvania were positioned in the ditch along the pike on the right of the photo. The large tree on the left of the pike stood witness to the battle. Careful examination reveals the entrance to the McPherson Farm on the right-hand side near the lowest point between the two ridges. (GNMP)

This view shows the conditon of the farm within days of the battle. There appears to be a lack of significant battle damage to the buildings. Brady and his assistant stand to the left of the original Breadon log kitchen. Trees obscure the stone section of the house. In the center stands the wagon shed and to the left of that is the imposing form of the McPherson barn. (GNMP)

This photo shows the appearance of the farm while the Slentzes were still in residence. To the right of the barn is the last of the old cherry trees that stood witness to the battle. The northern lean-to has been added and there are cows in the fenced area around the barn. The condition of the roof of the barn indicates that it may date to 1863. The wagon shed has been reoriented to face east (perpendicular to the original). A two-story frame house now stands where the original Breadon stone section once stood. Beyond the house stands Herbst Woods, still grovelike in appearance suggesting that animals may still graze there. (William H. Tipton, early 1880s GNMP).

This detail of the top photograph shows the poor condition of the McPherson barn some twenty years after the battle. A large lean-to shed has been attached to the north end of the barn almost completely obscuring the stone wall which still rises to the gable. The condition of the roof suggests that it may pre-date the battle.

Photo showing the dilapidated condition of the barn in 1905. The stable doors have fallen off, as has much of the original 1880s siding. Note the thickness of the north wall, which appears to be over 4' thick. The monument to John Reynolds stands in the distance. (William H. Tipton, 1905—GNMP)

This view shows the north wall of the barn after the Kappes rebuild. Most prominent is the concrete foundation. The ventilator embrasures are false and do not actually go through the wall. The gable siding has been painted to match the stone while the new metal roof has been adorned with lighting arrestors. (William H. Tipton, spring 1918, Annual Reports, Gettysburg National Military Park Commission)

View of the McPherson barn from the site of the original house. The mound in the immediate foreground marks the original stone foundation of the Breadon house. Close examinaton reveals some of the original stones lying about in the vicinity. The pile of bricks marks the place where the Breadon kitchen fireplace once stood. In all likelihood these are bricks original to the 1797 fireplace. The south wall has been partially rebuilt up to the gable and completely rebuilt from the gable to the roof line. The louvered openings in the stable area were rebuilt and reset. Ventilator embrasures have been added to replicate the original and new stone ramp walls and foundations have been rebuilt under the west lean-tos. The stable doors have been removed, straightened and re-hung while the hardware was restored and reinstalled. The forbay has been reframed using the methods of the time and all siding has been whitewashed. The roof has been replaced. It is unclear whether the stable fencing was replaced at the time of the restoration. Its condition suggests that it is probably not much more than twenty years old. (Author's Collection)

View of the northwest corner of the barn showing the rebuilt west lean-tos. Note that the doors have been moved back to their original location closer to the western façade of the building and that the siding has been correctly oriented vertically on the north lean-to and horizontally on the south lean-to. (Author's Collection)

Chapter 7

RETREAT THROUGH THE TOWN

"...dashing and flying...in every direction..."

DURING THE RETREAT the Bucktail brigade lost much of its cohesiveness and fell in with the rest of the First and Eleventh Corps mobs filling the streets of Gettysburg. Catherine Foster, a resident of Gettysburg, remembered the sight of the panicky Federal troops: "[The Federals] turned toward the town dashing and flying over fences and fields in every direction, like a shower of meteors. The artillery began to play and the shells to whiz over our heads."[254]

Colonel Charles S. Wainwright was among those retreating through the town. He recalled that

> the streets of the town were filled with the troops of the two corps. There was very little order amongst them, save that the Eleventh took one side of the street and we the other; brigades and divisions were pretty well mixed up. Still the men were not panic stricken; most of them were talking and joking.

Making his way along, Colonel Wainwright came upon the man whose troops had gotten in the way of his guns earlier in the day:

> As I pushed through the crowd as rapidly as possible, I came across General Rowley, who was in command of

---

254. Catherine Foster, "The Story of the Battle: By A Citizen Whose Home Was Pierced By Shells," *Gettysburg Compiler,* June 29 & July 6, 1904.

the Third Division. He was very talkative, claiming that he was in command of the corps. I tried to reason with him, showing that Wadsworth and several others ranked him; but soon finding that he was drunk, I rode on to the top of the Cemetery Hill, the existence of which I now learned for the first time. Whether Rowley would have handled his division any better had he been sober I have my doubts . . . .[255]

Sanford N. Boyden of Company A, 149th Pennsylvania, also recalled his experiences during the retreat through town:

From the time we left Seminary ridge until we reached the town we marched on the left of the Fairfield road. When we reached the town we took up the 1st street we came to leading to Cemetery Hill. The Rebs had got into the town before we did at least the houses were occupied by their sharpshooters and all the way from Seminary ridge to the town a Rebel column marched on either side of us a firing at us and we at them as fast as we could load and fire. I saw several good men killed or wounded while going up this street by Rebels shooting from the windows. Several of Co. A. 149PV were taken prisoner in the street.[256]

Simon Hubler became separated from the 143rd Pennsylvania during the retreat and soon found himself running for his life: "Near the entrance to the town of Gettysburg our regiment became pretty well broken up, and I presently found myself alone."[257] Moving down a side street he met up with a comrade of the 6th Wisconsin, who was also in search of his regiment and the prospect of safety. As the two traveled along they were spotted by some Rebels who demanded, "Halt, you Yankee sons of bitches!" Having no interest in becoming prisoners, Hubler and his comrade turned and sprinted for the Baltimore Pike. Shots rang out and one of the balls grazed Hubler's left ear and continued on striking the Midwesterner in the back of the head killing him instantly. Hubler

255. Allen Nevins, Diary of Battle, 237.
256. Sanford N. Boyden to R. E. Gamble, March 15, 1906.
257. Simon Hubler Account.

watched in horror as the man's brains oozed from his head. Just then a second ball struck Hubler's cartridge box. The concussion of the impact convinced Hubler that he had been shot through the hip. Upon examination, he found he could still run and so continued on in haste. Next he observed a Rebel taking aim at one of his comrades from behind a house. He thought to himself, "If only I had a load in my gun you wouldn't shoot one of our boys." Glancing to the right, he saw another Rebel thinking the same of Hubler but who was already busy ramming a ball into his musket and looking at him in a "most ferocious" manner. Without hesitation and before the Rebel could shoulder his weapon, he ducked out of sight. Further along the Baltimore Pike while passing a barn near Cemetery Hill, he was surprised to hear someone shout his name. It turned out to be Sydney Telle of Company I, 143rd Pennsylvania, who had been badly wounded in the left arm. Hubler aided his comrade by dressing the wound with his handkerchief and giving him a drink from his canteen. After finding him a comfortable place to lie in the barn, Hubler then went about exploring the building in search of hidden plunder. There he came across the knapsack of a New York artillery-man. The owner being absent, Hubler appropriated the man's tobacco, writing paper, and shell jacket, of which he quickly removed the red stripes and slipped it on. Hubler remained in the safety of the barn aiding his comrade until the morning of July 2.[258]

Sergeant James Rutter of the 143rd Pennsylvania, who had earlier rescued his wounded captain at the McPherson Farm, was just coming out of the private residence where he had taken him for aid when he saw some Federal soldiers dart in front of him. Startled, he yelled after them to inquire what their hurry was. "Look back and you'll find out!" was the response. "Sure enough, there were the Johnnies right onto me. 'No Libby Prison for me!' I thought, and I ran a race down an alley, through the fields, and at last came up to the old cemetery, where the whole runaway Eleventh Corps had massed. I slept that night in the cemetery, with a grave for a pillow, and never slept sounder."[259]

Captain Jones of the 150th Pennsylvania was able to keep his fleeing company in some order by filing them through the southern end

---

258. Ibid. Telle does not appear on the 143rd Pennsylvania's roster of killed and wounded.
259. "Sgt. James Rutter: Gettysburg Hero," *Sunday Independent*, May 28, 1989.

of town until they were ordered to halt by a Rebel officer. Private Terence O'Connor coolly took aim at the Rebel and bringing him down was heard to say, "We take no orders from the likes of you!"[260]

James W. Marshall of Company D, 150th Pennsylvania, remembered his actions upon the departure of the Federal batteries from Seminary Ridge: "We placed the Seminary between us and the rebels coming from the east. We turned south on a street where there was a large wooden pump with a long crooked handle, but before we reached the end of the street, the rebs were upon us. We got over a fence and ran south out of the ditch to Culp's Hill [Cemetery Hill], where we found Capt. Jones, of Co. B . . . ." Others remembered that "many hair-breadth escapes were made by leaping fences, crossing gardens, or passing through shops and dwellings, in order to reach streets to which the pursuing forces had not yet penetrated."[261]

Sergeant William R. Ramsey of Company F, 150th Pennsylvania, remembered:

> When I came through the town the houses were shut up, so far as I saw, except one, which stood on a street which ran at a right angle to the main thoroughfare. The house stood back having a large yard in front. An old man and woman and a young girl were busy bringing water from the pump or well, which was in the back yard, and serving it to all who asked for it, some half dozen of us got a drink there and before we could regain the main street, four of the party were shot down by rebel skirmishers who had come into the town on the east side and were posted behind the steps firing at every bluecoat they saw.[262]

Doctor James Fulton of the 143rd Pennsylvania was busy working on the wounded inside St. Xavier Catholic Church when he heard a great commotion outside the church:

> I went to the front into the street to see what was really going on. The first thing I knew a Confederate Major

260. Thomas Chamberlin, *History of the One Hundred and Fiftieth Pennsylvania*, 137.
261. Thomas Chamberlin, "Address at the Dedication of Monument, 150th Regiment Infantry," in John P. Nicholson, *Pennsylvania at Gettysburg*, 2 Vols. (Harrisburg, Pennsylvania: State Printer, 1904), 2:745.
262. Letter of Sergeant William R. Ramsey to Colonel J. B. Bachelder, April 16, 1883. *The Bachelder Papers*, 2:958.

tapped me on the shoulder and said I was his prisoner. I asked him what was to be done. He told me where I would find Gen. A. P. Hill and report to him. I did so. The General asked me if we did not have a good many sick and wounded. I told him we had, not only our own men but theirs also. He politely told me to go back and do the best I could for them.[263]

What was left of the Bucktail brigade moved through town under a "destructive fire," taking a defensive position behind a stone wall on the southwestern slope of Cemetery Hill between 5:00 and 6:00 P.M.[264] Thomas Chamberlin of the 150th Pennsylvania recalled the events of that evening:

> By five o'clock the troops of the First Corps were in position on Cemetery Hill, to the left of Steinwehr's division of the Eleventh Corps, and somewhat to his rear. The men of the 150th were at first gathered in two groups of nearly equal size, within a short distance of each other, but each ignorant of the other's proximity, and each supposing itself to be all that was left of the regiment. The true state of the case was soon discovered, however, and the fusion of the two bodies was the occasion of much satisfaction.[265]

Major Musser of the 143rd Pennsylvania did what he could to reorganize his wrecked regiment. Recalling their arrival on Cemetery Hill, he remarked:

> We sat down to rest, but could not sit still. Officers and men shook hands in silence, great tear drops standing in their undaunted eyes, as they thought of the dead and wounded left in the hands of the cursed Rebels. We were almost afraid to ask each other where the rest of our regt. were, we knew most of them were either killed or wounded . . . Weary and hungry, in line of battle, we lay upon our arms and slept.[266]

263. James Fulton, "Gettysburg Reminiscences."
264. O.R., Vol. XXVII, pt. 1, p. 336.
265. Thomas Chamberlin, "Address at the Dedication."
266. Musser to D. Ribu, December 10, 1863.

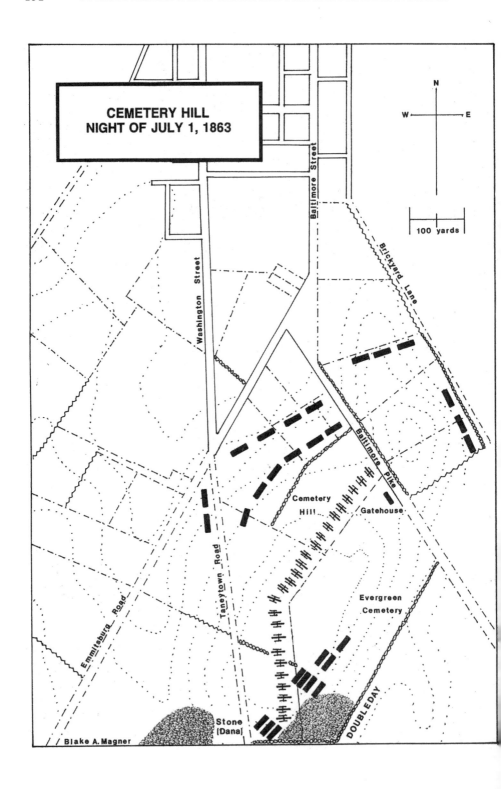

**CEMETERY HILL
NIGHT OF JULY 1, 1863**

N

W — E

100 yards

Baltimore Street

Brickyard Lane

Washington Street

Baltimore Pike

Cemetery
Hill

Gatehouse

Taneytown Road

Emmitsburg Road

Evergreen
Cemetery

DOUBLEDAY

Stone
[Dana]

Blake A. Magner

First Lieutenant Jacob F. Slagle of Company D, 149th Pennsylvania, stated: "We got to the cemetery between four and five o'clock and were busy getting the men together and taking new positions. There was a battery just at the top of the hill in the cemetery and we rallied around that . . . . The 3rd Division occupied the side of the hill in the cemetery and to the left."[267]

Most of the men of the Second Brigade had not had food or water all day. William Wright of the 149th Pennsylvania remembered, "I was nearly dead for water. I happened to see some water a lieing [sic] on a rock that had geathered [sic] the evening before when it rained. I was so near to give out that I lay down and drank off that rock. You may no [sic] that I was dry."[268]

Patrick DeLacy of the 143rd Pennsylvania suffered similarly: "I am nearly famished with hunger and my lips are almost cracking from thirst. I find a small stream and am about to take a drink when I notice a soldiers head touching the water. He is dead, with his head hanging only by shreds."[269]

As evening passed, those who had become detached from the brigade slowly rejoined their commands. Two great armies would continue to converge on Gettysburg throughout the night. Six hours earlier, Stone's Bucktail Brigade had arrived on the field with 1,317 officers and men. Only now, as the sun began its descent toward the horizon and roll was called, could they realize the magnitude of their loss. In the course of the day's horrible action, the brigade had lost 105 men killed, 462 wounded, and 279 missing or captured, a total loss of 848 men or 64 percent. The brigade had been new to combat when it passed over Seminary Ridge earlier that day, but six hours of brutal attacks and counterattacks had helped to make them seasoned veterans. At no time had they wavered in the face of attack when there was any possibility of holding their ground. Only after being pressed by overwhelming numbers and confronted with the loss of the entire command was there talk of withdrawal. It was quite clear that they had in fact "Come to stay."

267. Letter of Jacob F. Slagle to his Brother, September 13, 1863. Copy GNMP.
268. William Wright to Mary Wright, July 7, 1863. Copy GNMP.
269. Patrick DeLacy, "Capt. DeLacy Describes Gettysburg Battle."

Chapter 8

July 2, 1863

"...gathering their strength for the final struggle."

THE BUCKTAILS REMAINED where they were through the night of July 1 and most of July 2. Sergeant William R. Ramsey of Company F, 150th Pennsylvania, described the brigade's position: "On our right were the woods in the Cemetery and the stone-wall enclosing them, on our left was the Taneytown road; I do not mean that our right or left touched either of these points, but we were between them. . . ."[270] Lieutenant Colonel John Musser, commanding the 143rd Pennsylvania, recalled that "on the morning of the 2nd we found ourselves supporting Battery C [Captain Wallace Hill's Battery C, 1st West Virginia Light Artillery] near the crest of the hill. About 8 o'clock, a little brisk cannonading occurred."[271] These were most likely the guns of Lieutenant Samuel Wallace's 2nd Rockbridge (Virginia) Artillery ranging in on Cemetery Hill from Seminary Ridge.[272] "With the exception of some skirmishing between the advanced posts and occasional artillery firing, the morning of Thursday, July 2, on this part of the field passed in comparative quiet," wrote Colonel Dana.[273]

While the Bucktails passed the morning on the southern slope of Cemetery Hill, Simon Hubler of the 143rd Pennsylvania, who had become separated from his regiment during the retreat the day before, was still caring for a wounded comrade in a barn on the southeastern edge of Gettysburg.

270. Letter of Sergeant William R. Ramsey to Colonel J. B. Bachelder, September 30, 1883. *The Bachelder Papers*, 2:971.
271. John Musser, Musser Papers, USAMHI. Copy GNMP.
272. Harry W. Phanz, *Gettysburg – Culp's Hill and Cemetery Hill* (Chapel Hill, 1993), 179.
273. O.R., Vol. XXVII, pt. 1, p. 336.

I stayed . . . in the barn all night and in the morning 12 men belonging to the 55th Ohio entered the barn for the purpose of sharp-shooting. The mini-balls were striking the barn at frequent intervals. The first thing these fellows did was to find and take my writing paper and tobacco, which I had hid, and then they proceeded to open fire on the enemy.

Along about eight or nine o'clock in the morning I looked out of an aperture between the beam of the barn and the wall supporting the barn, and saw two Confederates running along the post and rail fence about 250 yards distant. I took deliberate aim at one of the men who was running, and fired. The man at whom I aimed fell forward on his face, while the other one hurried away as fast as he could run. I do not know whether I killed this man or not, because others were shooting at the same time.[274]

Hubler spent the remainder of the morning in the barn accompanied by the detail from the 55th Ohio. Together they traded shots with the Rebels occupying the houses in the southern portion of town. At some point, the lieutenant commanding the Ohioans requested a volunteer to carry a note back to his regiment a few hundred yards distant on Cemetery Hill. "The men who were under the lieutenant hesitated about taking the note, and I [Hubler] volunteered to take it."[275]

I took the note and ran in a zig-zag fashion toward the wall where the 55th Ohio regiment was stationed. When I reached the wall I walked along in front of it for some distance, when someone shouted, "Say you Pennsylvanian, you had better jump over here or you'll get plugged."

During my run the bullets had sung uncomfortably near, so I hastily followed the advice which was given me and jumped over the wall.

---

274. Simon Hubler Account. It seems likely, given his description and the proximity of the 55th Ohio, that the barn Hubler and his comrade spent the night in was probably the present-day Dobbins house.
275. Ibid.

Evidently the note contained a request for more men because the major immediately detailed a squad of 12 more men, and inquired of me how they would find their way to the proper place.

I told the detail to follow me and sprang over the wall, and running zig-zag fashion we all safely reached the barn.[276]

Upon returning to the barn, Hubler decided it would be best to get his comrade back into the Federal lines and the care of a surgeon. Retracing his steps he helped his wounded comrade over the wall in front of the 55th Ohio and continued on until finding a surgeon. "I watched them remove the bullet from Telley's arm and . . . hurried away to find my regiment. I found my regiment lying behind the cemetery."[277]

Colonel Dana described what happened next:

In the afternoon, a severe engagement occurred on our left, and simultaneously a cannonade opened between our batteries on Cemetery Hill and those of the enemy. Later in the day this brigade, with the First, moved at a double-quick and under a sharp fire about a half mile to the left and front, to re-enforce that portion of the line. The One hundred and forty-ninth and One hundred and fiftieth Regiments, under Captains Glenn and Jones, were here advanced some 600 yards, until they encountered the enemy's pickets, and in the morning rejoined the brigade, bringing with them two pieces of artillery and caissons recovered from the field.[278]

At about 6:00 P.M., the Bucktails were double-quicked to the left, down the Taneytown Road, to a position behind the Leister house. Here they were halted and bayonets were fixed for a charge but the Rebels were repulsed before the order to charge was given.[279] Though the Bucktails played little role in repulsing Wright's

---

276. Ibid.
277. Ibid.
278. O.R., Vol. XXVII, pt. 1, pp. 336, 340, 348. Probably the Napoleons of Gulian V. Weir's Battery C, 5th U.S. Artillery.
279. Thomas Chamberlin, *History of the One Hundred and Fiftieth Pennsylvania*, 149.

Georgians from the crest of Cemetery Ridge, they did arrive in comparatively fresh condition. As such, the 149th and 150th Pennsylvania were pushed forward to picket along the Emmittsburg Road in the vicinity of the Codori farm: "The 150th deployed as skirmishers, the 149th supporting them."[280] Thomas Chamberlin of the 150th Pennsylvania recalled, "The regiment continued its advance in the growing darkness until the right impinged on the Emmittsburg road, a little to the left of the Codori House. . . ."[281] There they were halted by Rebel skirmishers on the high ground beyond the road. Sergeant William R. Ramsey of Company F, 150th Pennsylvania, recalled that during the night he "got water for a good many wounded rebels [and] in talking with them found they were mostly Georgians."[282] John Nesbit of Company D, 149th Pennsylvania, wrote:

We spent the night, when not on duty, carrying water from the well at the Codori house to the wounded of both armies. It was a long and sleepless night. The cries and moans of the wounded and dying, the close proximity of the rebel pickets and the general uncertainty as to the result of the fighting and the real situation, kept our boys awake and nervous.[283]

William Wright of the 149th Pennsylvania also remembered the picket duty: "We picketed on the battlefield wheare [sic] the battle was hot the 2nd. I never want to picket on an other battlefield. Theare [sic] was wounded men a laying on the field a crying for water all night and I couldn't give them any."[284] While on picket duty, Sergeant George Hopkins of Company F, 150th Pennsylvania, happened upon a wounded Floridian who told Hopkins that before the battle they had been instructed by their officers not to take any

280. Letter of Sergeant William R. Ramsey to Colonel J. B. Bachelder, April 16, 1883. *The Bachelder Papers*, 2:950. Perhaps because of the severe loss of officers on July 1, very few accounts exist relating to the advance of the 149th and 150th to the Emmitsburg Road. The captains who now commanded the regiments were unaccustomed to making such reports and therefore did not give the kind of detail necessary in describing their movements and activities. The one man capable of such reports, Colonel Dana, for some reason chose to stay back on Cemetery Ridge with the 143rd Pennsylvania.
281. Thomas Chamberlin, *History of the One Hundred and Fiftieth Pennsylvania*, 150.
282. Letter of Sergeant William R. Ramsey to Colonel J. B. Bachelder, April 16, 1883. *The Bachelder Papers*, 2:950.
283. Richard Matthews, *The 149th Pennsylvania*, 98.
284. William Wright to Mary Wright, July 7, 1863. Copy GNMP.

prisoners because Pennsylvania troops were "killing all captives." Hopkins went on to say that, "He seemed greatly surprised, on learning that we were Pennsylvanians, [and] that we did not despatch the wounded."[285]

Back on Cemetery Ridge the men of the 143rd Pennsylvania pondered the events of the last two days and anxiously speculated their fate tomorrow. Patrick DeLacy recalled:

> When sleep came there was not a man in the 143rd who wasn't expecting the most spectacular battle to come either on the morrow or the following day. All sorts of reports were coming to the camp on the hillside and there wasn't a man among us who didn't expect to be plunged into the fiercest kind of fighting before another twenty-four hours.[286]

John Musser of the 143rd Pennsylvania remembered that "in line of battle without anything to eat, we again lay upon our arms and slept. . . . We rested but during the night there was great activity among the artillery. They were gathering their strength for the final struggle."[287]

The sounds of the wounded that night kept many from sleeping. Simon Hubler was among the restless:

> During the night of the 2nd I heard someone cry for water out in front of our position. The boys told me I'd get plugged, but I took the risk and proceeded with a canteen of water out in front of the line in the direction of the cry. Presently I came across the object of my search, and found him to be a Confederate soldier mortally wounded. I gave him all the water I had in my canteen . . . The next morning our skirmishers found him dead.

---

285. Thomas Chamberlin, *History of the One Hundred and Fiftieth Pennsylvania*, 150.
286. Patrick DeLacy, "Capt. DeLacy Describes Gettysburg Battle."
287. John Musser, Musser Papers, USAMHI. Copy GNMP.

Chapter 9

JULY 3, 1863

"...the very air was alive with iron hail."

ABOUT 8:00 A.M. on July 3, the 143rd Pennsylvania was rejoined by the 149th and 150th Pennsylvania when they were relieved by a fresh skirmish line. Together they lay along Cemetery Ridge just south and east of what would soon become known as the Copse of Trees. In their immediate rear was Captain James McKay Rorty's Battery B, 1st New York Light. John Musser remembered:

> At daylight we again found ourselves supporting another battery, General Doubleday directed us to throw up breast works, by gathering rails, stones, and piling these in front of us. We worked quietly but steadily . . . the boys were prospecting around, some lay lazily on the ground, some sleeping, boiling coffee.[288]

Musser remembered that later the early afternoon air erupted in flames: "Two solitary guns were fired in quick succession. It was the signal for the attack, there was a grand rush among officers and men for their positions."[289] In his Official Report, John Musser said:

> In the afternoon the enemy opened on us. We had not taken our position yet, but lay some distance in rear. While doing so a shell struck in Company D, instantly

288. Ibid.
289. Ibid.

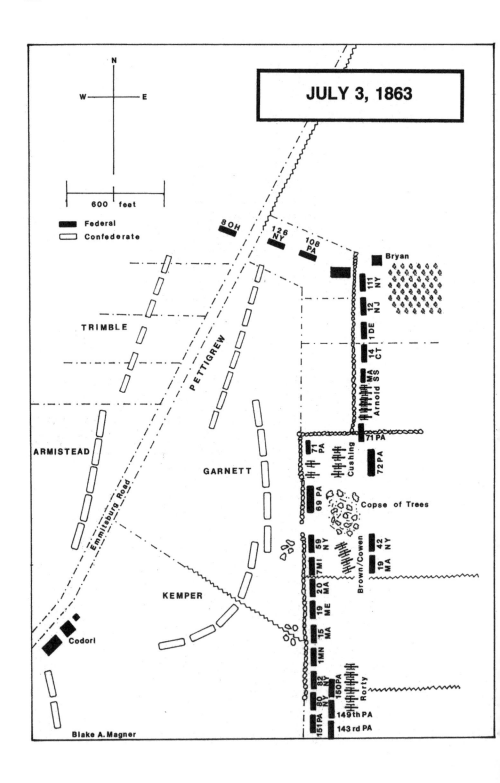

JULY 3, 1863

N

W——E

600 feet

■ Federal
☐ Confederate

8 OH

126 NY

108 PA

Bryan

111 NY

12 NJ

1 DE

14 CT

MA SS

Arnold

71 PA

71 PA

Cushing

72 PA

69 PA

Copse of Trees

TRIMBLE

PETTIGREW

GARNETT

59 NY

7 MI

42 NY

Brown/Cowen

19 MA

ARMISTEAD

Emmitsburg Road

20 MA

19 ME

KEMPER

15 MA

1 MN

82 NY

150 PA

Rorty

Codori

80 NY

149th PA

151 PA

143 rd PA

Blake A. Magner

killing 1 and wounding others. I then ordered my men up to the breastwork, after which no shell struck among the men, but a number were wounded with pieces. We remained under the concentrated fire of several batteries, but all proved useless; they could not silence our batteries, and made the attack with infantry, farther to our right. The column in front [Stannard's Vermonters] swung round upon the flank of the enemy. Our line did not move from the support of the battery.[290]

Musser went on to describe the Rebel artillery fire: "For 3 hours the earth shook, the very air was alive with iron hail. Such a storm of shell and solid shot was never heard before. No place was safe."[291]

John Nesbitt of Company D, 149th Pennsylvania, described the bombardment:

The cannonading was incessant and terrific. We had no protection whatever, but lay in the hot sun, under the fire of both armies, flattened out and hugging the ground, awaiting further developments.

The battery in our rear was about 20 feet back; their line of fire was no more than three feet above us and the . . . concussion was so great that the grass between and in front of our men flattened to the ground with every discharge.[292]

Before long, Simon Hubler recalled, "the artillery fire from our batteries slackened until only here and there a gun boomed defiance to the enemy."[293] Hubler was peering through the smoke toward Seminary Ridge when he saw the Rebels advance into the open: "Hello, boys, here comes a charge. The Confederates came . . . directly toward our position."

Pickett's charge advanced in good order toward the Copse of Trees atop Cemetery Ridge. When the Rebels came within 600 yards, the Bucktails opened on them. Across the fields some 10,500

---

290. O.R., Vol. XXVII, pt. 1, p. 340.
291. John Musser, Musser Papers, USAMHI. Copy GNMP.
292. J. W. Nesbit, "Recollections of Pickett's Charge," *National Tribune*, November 16, 1916.
293. Simon Hubler Account.

Rebels moved obliquely to the left. "The din was awful," Hubler remembered. "We could see the fighting only indistinctly because of obstructions in the way, and because of the powder smoke."[294] Patrick DeLacy of the 143rd Pennsylvania recalled:

> We are firing as fast as we can and fairly riddling one of the detachments of [Pickett's Confederates'] magnificent line. We keep up pelting at this force. I can see no end to the right nor left. . . . Our regiment gets the order to cease firing. Vermont regiments are passing just below us ranging into the defense line. The officers of these regiments, fearful that our shots will find marks among those boys shout to us on the hillside to stop firing. The command then comes to us from our officers. . . . The clash now comes. The Vermont boys and the other boys refuse to yield an inch. Men are now fighting within feet of each other. Muskets are being used as clubs. On the hillside we are cheering like mad. "Give it to them," we cry, waving our hats.[295]

John W. Nesbit of the 149th Pennsylvania recalled the movement of Stannard's Vermonters:

> While this fighting was going on there was nothing between the right of our brigade and the hand-to-hand contest except the cluster of trees. The noise and the din of fighting was awful; and while we were perfectly quiet and safe, we did not know what to expect. The Vermont brigade which was part of our line, finding that Gen. Wilcox with his division had become detached from the main column, moved out front and to the left; engaged Wilcox; captured a number of men, and dispersed the balance. This, with the death of Armistead and their failure to make a positive break in our lines, ended the contest.[296]

294. Ibid.
295. Patrick DeLacy, "Capt. DeLacy Describes Gettysburg Battle."
296. John W. Nesbit, "Recollections of Pickett's Charge."

Simon Hubler remembered: "We soon saw small bodies of Confederates retreating, and then larger masses which hurried back, broken and disorganized . . . Pickett's charge was over . . . and during the remaining hours of daylight the firing was desultory."[297]

John Nesbit of the 149th Pennsylvania described the aftermath of the charge:

> After it was known that the fight was over I walked around about the trees, and about 50 feet from the left of our line I found the ground practically covered with dead and wounded men, both blue and gray. It was the same down to the stone fence and angle, and over the fence down to the pike the ground was apparently covered with men in gray, dead and wounded. It appeared to me that I could have walked on the bodies of the dead and wounded men to the fence and down to the Emmitsburg Pike. Evidence of the terrible bloody fighting appeared everywhere, but I was not permitted to investigate further . . .[298]

Lieutenant Colonel John Musser of the 143rd Pennsylvania recalled how the Bucktails spent the night of July 3:

> Another night we lay down upon our arms and slept, while others watched. None of us had eaten anything, since the morning of the 1st, when they stacked their haversacks for the Rebels.
>
> At daylight we were relieved. We could go to the rear. Our supplies had been ordered to Westminster the 1st day and none present yet. I sent some men from each company to beg. It was raining but they soon returned with arms full of meat, bread, coffee, and sugar. We had a good breakfast. I enjoyed it. Not a gun was fired on the 4th. Each army occupied its own position and the dead and wounded lay on the field uncared for.[299]

---

297. Simon Hubler Account.
298. John W. Nesbit, "Recollections of Pickett's Charge."
299. John Musser, Musser Papers, USAMHI. Copy GNMP.

The repulse of the ill-fated Pickett-Pettigrew-Trimble Charge signaled the end of the battle of Gettysburg. According to a Bucktail, "We remained on the line until evening, when we were ordered back to the Taneytown Road and camped there until July 5th when we followed the army back to Virginia."[300]

That Stone's brigade fought gallantly at Gettysburg cannot be disputed. The controversy surrounding the naming of the Bucktail Brigade notwithstanding, the Bucktails did more to solidify their reputation at Gettysburg than in all previous conflicts combined. Colonel Dawes of the Iron Brigade paid the Bucktails a high compliment by saying, "Their conduct was more than heroic, it was glorious."[301] But Lieutenant Colonel John D. Musser may have said it best when he wrote, "All are worthy of the highest praise, and [I] believe that history will record it, as one of the most stubbornly contested battles of the war."[302]

300. J. W. Nesbit, "Recollections of Pickett's Charge," National Tribune, November 16, 1916.
301. Rufus R. Dawes, Service with the Sixth Wisconsin Volunteers, 174.
302. Musser to D. Ribu, December 10, 1863.

Chapter 10

STONE'S CASUALTIES ON THE MCPHERSON FARM

"...at this point of woods had been a fiercely contested battle."

BY LATE AFTERNOON of July 1, 1863, casualties littered the McPherson Farm and surrounding area. Hundreds, perhaps thousands of dead and wounded soldiers lay on the field. The Federal First Corps was decimated and would never recover from its losses in Herbst Woods and on the McPherson Farm. Heth's, Pender's, and part of Rodes's Confederate divisions were mauled on these fields and were never the same. The Bucktails held their position on the McPherson Farm at a critical period of the battle. That they stubbornly refused to withdrawal was partly to blame for their high casualties. The table below illustrates the total loss incurred for the gallant Second Brigade on July 1, 1863:

Command	Strength	Losses (K-W-MC)	Percent Loss
Stone			
143 Pa	465	250 (20-139-91)[303]	53.7
149 Pa	450	335 (52-172-111)[304]	74.4
150 Pa	400	263 (33-151-77)[305]	65.7
Totals	**1315**	**848**	**64.4**[306]

303. The 143rd Pennsylvania lost one wounded on July 2 as well as one wounded and one killed on July 3.
304. The 149th Pennsylvania lost one man killed on July 3.
305. The 150th Pennsylvania lost an additional two men, one killed and one wounded, in Company A on July 3.
306. Busey and Martin, *Regimental Strengths and Loses at Gettysburg*, 28.

Those that were not killed outright painfully crawled and dragged themselves through the fields in search of water, shade, and medical assistance. Many of those who were able to walk found refuge from the elements in the McPherson buildings. The rest lay where they had fallen, calling on comrades for help. Some may have prayed for the passage of a quick death.

Captain Francis B. Jones of Company G, 149th Pennsylvania, was one of those left behind on the McPherson Farm. He had been wounded twice in the left leg and could not be carried off when the Bucktails retired. He later recalled his ordeal following the collapse of the Federal line:

> As soon as our troops had retired, the enemy came over that part of the field, marching in its line of battle, until regiment after regiment had passed on towards Gettysburg town and beyond it, where the fighting was still going on. As each line of battle came to where I was, the Captains ordered their men to open ranks, so as not to injure me as they passed by. After the infantry, came the Artillery at full gallop on the turnpike. I saw there was danger of them getting off the road into the low part where I was. Also I saw the Southern Army's stragglers were going over the field, robbing the wounded, so I made up my mind I would try crawling about 125 yards to McPherson's barn, a safer place. It was slow and tedious work, as I was loaded down with my sword, revolver, rubber blanket, canteen, tin cup, a little tea and sugar, and a few broken-up hardbread. When I was about in the middle of the plowed field next to the barn, I saw a rebel soldier with a gun on his shoulder, in charge of a disarmed Union soldier with a bucktail in his hat (of the 150th Pa. Regiment). I called them to come to me. The rebel said he had been sent to the rear of his army with this one man as a prisoner. I knew that was not so. They were both only too glad to get away from the battle. I told the rebel I wanted him and his prisoner to help me over to the barn. He demurred very much, but the Union man told him they must do it as I was a Captain of his

own brigade, and he was going to see that I got under cover. I got them to stoop down until I could get an arm around of their necks, and they did carry me into McPherson's barn and placed me on some straw in a horse stall. I found Col. Roy Stone lying in the next stall, wounded in the hip; also my 2nd Lieut. John T. Miller, with his jaw broken by a bullet, together with several men of my Company, together with many others of our regiment.[307]

Also of Company G, 149th Pennsylvania, was William L. Antis who "was wounded on the First Day's fight and remained on the field for several days before being found and cared for."[308]

William L. Perry of the 150th Pennsylvania was wounded in the leg around 3:00 P.M. on July 1, and left on the field. He described his experiences on the afternoon and evening of the First Day: "As I lay by the roadside I had plenty of company and we were talking and argueing [sic] until 10 o'clock at night without the least hard feelings."[309]

Mr. J. F. McKendrick, an Adams County resident who lived in the area, "was among the first to reach the line of the first day's battle and finding the wounded lying where they fell, without food or water, joined in ministering to their needs and remaining until late in the night of July 2nd."[310]

With darkness closing in and the McPherson Farm now behind Rebel lines, it was safe for the collection of the dead and wounded. Details were arranged for this purpose. One of those was led by J. A. Walker of the 45th Georgia who policed the area between Herbst Woods and the Seminary:

> I first came upon the ground fought over by McGowan's South Carolina troops. Many of his dead were still unburied and a few wounded sitting about fence corners . . . We buried a great many in this field and about sundown came to the corner of the Reynolds [Herbst]

---

307. Francis B. Jones, *Chronicles of Francis Bacon Jones*.
308. *Raftsman's Journal*, Clearfield, PA, April 15, 1914.
309. Diary of William F. Perry. Copy GNMP.
310. *Raftsman's Journal*, Clearfield, PA, April 15, 1914.

woods, where General Reynolds had been killed that day. I rested for a while on this fence, very near the corner where it turns towards Herr's Tavern . . . at this point of woods had been a fiercely contested battle. General Reynolds, whose statue is in the National Cemetery here, was killed under this large oak. Many of General Archer's Tennesseans were captured in these woods and the trees today give evidence of war in their shattered limbs and perforated trunks . . . It was now night and I could no longer see to work. Very near this place is a small farm house . . . It is a few hundred yards north of the "Reynolds" oak. This farm house was the scene of one of the bloodiest battles of the war. Taken and retaken, riddled by bullets, filled with dead and dying, the very cows and horses shot down by stray bullets, and yet not materially damaged. Seeing a light in it I went in to see if my services were needed. I found it filled with Federal dead and wounded. I made known my business to them, when they informed me of their having been already captured and left to be treated for their wounds. Physicians for both armies were in attendance, and finding my services not needed I started for the door.[311]

The house referred to was the McPherson house. John Slentz, tenant at the time of the battle, petitioned the government after the battle for damages incurred during the fight. Part of his claim was for seven head of horned cattle that were killed and two that were wounded. These were apparently the cows that Walker would later see while visiting the farm. Walker went on to describe the remainder of the night:

> My labors were now over and as it was near midnight I bivouacked my men in the yard, spreading down our blankets along the ground near the pike and where the fence now stands. Sleep was out of the question to me, and while the men were snoring soundly I was left alone

---

311. J. A. Walker, "Soul Stirring Incidents," *Philadelphia Weekly Times*, in Gettysburg Newspaper Clippings, 6, "Relating to the Battle," GNMP, 14.

in my meditations. With my face upturned to the sky and looking at the stars, it fell to the lot of a little calf to speak more eloquently than all the rest of the war's sacrifices. The mother of the little dumb beast was killed by a stray shot during the day. Evidently a pet of the household, it wandered about the whole of the night, bleating and moaning piteously for its dam. There was not a sound on earth except the weary stepping of its tired limbs, and when it came over to where I was lying and touched its cold nose to my hand I felt that it was indeed a cruel fate that demanded of the brute sucking its share of trouble.[312]

Walker does not specifically mention going into the barn and tending any wounded there though it is clear that it was filled with the dead and dying of both armies. It is curious that he noted the presence of surgeons from both armies working in the house since the preponderance of the evidence suggests a complete lack of any medical attention on the farm until the next day, July 2. Unfortunately most of the help that did arrive on July 2 had no medical training and could do little more than provide water and emotional comfort. Those with medical training were soon escorted to the rear.

Arriving on July 2 as a Rebel prisoner, Lieutenant John Q. Carpenter of Company E, 150th Pennsylvania, was permitted to assist in the care of the wounded of his regiment. Throughout the day, Carpenter aided in the burial of the dead and the removal of the wounded to the McPherson barn.

Posing as a member of the hospital corps by wearing a white piece of cloth around his arm, Lieutenant R. B. Beath of the 88th Pennsylvania was able to avoid capture and was allowed passage to the rear to assist in the care of the wounded:

[U]pon reaching McPherson's barn he found it full of bleeding and mangled soldiers in a most distressed and sickening condition, without a surgeon to dress their festering wounds and bind up their splintered bones. Many of the unfortunate were so shockingly lacerated that they

---

312. Ibid.

were unable to move, being in some cases glued to the floor by the blood flowing from their gaping wounds congealing in pools under them, and all were in torment, suffering from their thirst and hunger. These pitiful cases awakened all the sympathy in the Lieutenant's heart, and he at once set to work to alleviate their sufferings.[313]

Captain Francis B. Jones of the 149th Pennsylvania who had been wounded and subsequently helped into the barn on July 1 described the arrival of a Federal surgeon on July 2:

On the 2nd of July, a Northern surgeon who was himself a prisoner, came into the barn. He looked at my leg, and when he saw it was black, he said mortification had set in and that it should be amputated at once to save my life. I asked him to get the necessary instruments and cut it off, but he made the excuse that he could not get any instruments and had to go off with the other prisoners to the rear of the rebel Army. (The enemy sent their guards around to gather up any man that could walk, and take these off as prisoners.) The surgeon removed the handkerchief I had tied around my leg the day before, and told me to keep the leg wet with cold water, which seemed impossible as I could not get out to the well for water. But fortunately for me, soon after that I saw a Dutchman, Private Heiner, of my Company, looking in the stable door. I called to him to inquire how he was wounded. He replied that he was not wounded at all, but he said, "Captain, I was so terribly frightened when the Company went into battle on the first of July, I crawled under a hay stack as we passed it." And he had just come out when I saw him at the stable door. I tied my white handkerchief around his arm as a badge, and told him he must tell the rebel guards, when they came around, that he was a hospital attendant and that he had to look after this whole barnful of wounded men. So I had him keep my tin quart

---

313. John D. Vautier, "At Gettysburg: The Eighty-Eighth Pennsylvania Infantry in the Battle," *The Press* (November 10, 1886) in Gettysburg Newspaper Clippings, "Relating to the Battle," 6:125.

cup filled with water, and I soaked my leg day and night with cold water. Much to my relief, the blood commenced to flow in the veins again, and in a few days the black look turned to blue then gradually to yellow, and as long as I remained quiet I was comparatively free of pain . . . During my stay in the barn, I saw and talked with a Lieutenant on the rebel General Stuart's staff . . . I saw he had a very poor sword belt, so I asked him to accept mine which was an excellent one. I had it made of bridle leather. He was glad to get the belt . . . .[314]

Following Pickett's doomed assault on July 3, Colonel Henry Morrow, commander of the 24th Michigan of the Iron Brigade which had fought so valiantly in Herbst Woods, confronted Rebel Brigadier General John B. Gordon requesting assistance for the wounded who lay uncared for on the First Day's field. Gordon graciously offered Colonel Morrow a detail of ambulances to bring in the wounded. Around dusk Morrow and 12 ambulances started from the town in the direction of his men lying about Herbst Woods and the fields to the east. It is possible that the ambulances never arrived, deciding instead to bring in the rest of Gordon's men north of the town. If they did arrive they did not attempt to bring in the wounded from the McPherson Farm and buildings because there were still plenty lying about uncared for two days later.

It seems odd that although many Federals and Confederates knew of the suffering on the McPherson Farm, no one sent any medical help. Perhaps the Federals were reluctant to send their surgeons into the uncertainty of working behind enemy lines. The Rebel surgeons were certainly busy enough plying their vocation in the town. Overlooking the McPherson Farm area meant that they were also forsaking the brave Mississippians, Virginians, and North Carolinians who had fought so hard to take the position and who now lay about the buildings praying for help. Ironically, when help did arrive it was from the civilian population and not the medical establishment.

One of the first to offer assistance may have been William

---

314. Francis B. Jones, *Chronicles of Francis Bacon Jones.*

McLean. The following unsigned article describes what he found upon his arrival:

> I was informed that men were suffering in the McPherson Barn, on the Chambersburg Pike. My good wife went to work, baked biscuits, prepared gruel and we gathered fresh Antwerp raspberries in our garden, and loaded up with as much as I could carry, I started, on foot of course, to the barn. As a civilian I must confess to a little trepidation in going to what was so recently the front, and hearing the firing of artillery, as the retreat was being followed up. There were parties engaged in burying the dead in the fields, where they fell. A dead soldier in blue was lying along the side of the turnpike, black and swollen from the heat and rain, disfigured beyond recognition. When I entered the barn it was crowded with the wounded of both armies some of them having fallen four days before and without having any food, except in some cases the little hardtack in their haversacks, and without any surgical attention to their wounds. There were so many of these wounded and so closely packed together, that I was obliged to tramp on some of them in distributing my supplies. You may imagine how pleased and grateful they were for this fresh food, in their famished and suffering condition. One of them told me that as he was lying on the field, Gen. Lee had given him a drink of water out of his canteen. Lee's headquarters were in this locality. Many of these poor fellows must have died afterwards from gangrene.[315]

A horrible scene presented itself to the civilians of Gettysburg upon leaving the shelter of their homes on July 4, 1863. About them lay the wreckage of two armies with nearly 170,000 armed combatants, who had struggled for possession of the ground for the previous three days.

---

315. Author Unknown, "The Days of Terror in 1863," in Gettysburg newspaper Clippings, "Relating to the Battle," 6:155.

All around us were evidences of a great battle. The wounded, the dying, all heaped together; horses had fallen ... with limbs shattered and torn-dead, wounded and bleeding-broken down artillery wagons, guns and knapsacks, cartridge boxes, capes, coats and shoes; indeed all the belongings of a soldier and the soldier himself, all lying ... as far as we could see. ...[316]

At least 51,000 soldiers, both Federal and Confederate, had fallen in the early July battle. The occupants of Gettysburg now had more than 10 times their number lying wounded and dead about the countryside. Professor Michael Jacobs of Pennsylvania College (now Gettysburg College) recalled:

[A]fter the battle, the field yet everywhere bore the fresh marks of the terrible struggle. The soil was yet red with the blood of the wounded and the slain, and large numbers of the dead of both armies were to be seen lying in the place where the fatal missiles struck them ... Trees were scarred and shattered, thousands of minie balls, of solid shot and shells, lay scattered over the ground ....[317]

Federal dead and wounded still lay unattended about the McPherson Farm and buildings. Visiting the area on July 4, Confederate artilleryman Lieutenant Robert Stiles recalled the condition of the Federal casualties:

The sights and smells that assailed us were simply indescribable—corpses swollen to twice their original size. Some of them actually burst asunder with the pressure of foul gases and vapors. I recall one feature never before noted, the shocking distension and protension of the eyeballs of the dead men and dead horses. Several human or unhuman corpses sat upright against a fence,

316. Fannie J. Buehler, *Recollections of the Rebel Invasion and One Woman's Experience during the Battle of Gettysburg* (Gettysburg, Pennsylvania: Star and Sentinel Print, 1900), 24-25.

317. Michael Jacobs, "Later Rambles Over the Field of Gettysburg," in *Administrative History, Gettysburg National Military Park and National Cemetery, Pennsylvania,* (United States Department of the Interior, National Park Service, 1991), 3.

with arms extended in the air and faces hideous with something very like a fixed leer, as if taking a fiendish pleasure in showing us what we essentially were and might at any moment become. The odors were nauseating, and so deadly that in a short time we were all sickened and were lying with our mouths close to the ground, most of us vomiting profusely.[318]

As if the painful death suffered during ferocious combat were not enough, many of these soldiers endured the further indignity of battlefield robbery. Because the Federal dead of Stone's brigade lay behind enemy lines until July 5, the Rebels had plenty of time to loot their bodies. Sergeant Thomas Meyer of the 148th Pennsylvania stated:

It was a rare occurrence to find one who had not been robbed by the battlefield bandit or robber of the dead. Generally the pockets were cut open and rifled through the incision . . . [B]attlefield robbers were well known by the large amounts of money they had, and the watches, pocketbooks, pocket knives and other valuable trinkets they had for sale after the battle.

By July 5 tourists had already begun to arrive on the field. One of them was a preacher from York Springs who recorded the following:

I started out Chambersburg Street on a tour of observation. In looking over the ground many little hillocks could be seen where the dead had been covered with earth just where they fell and died. In the Theological Seminary I found all the rooms filled with the wounded. Going beyond I passed over the open ground in the direction of a large stone barn on the Chambersburg pike. The landscape here was thickly dotted with those same little hillocks in every direction. As I neared the

318. Robert Stiles, *Four Years Under Marse Robert* (New York: The Neale Publishing Company, 1903; reprint, Dayton, Ohio: Morningside, 1977), 219-220.

stone barn and was gazing around indifferently, I heard a voice calling and a man looking over the side of a pig sty. He beckoned to me with his hand and as I approached cried out: "For God's sake, Chaplain, come and help us; there's no one here to do it." When I examined the situation I found that the barn above and below, the wagon shed, the tenant house, the pig sty, and the open barnyard were all crowded with badly wounded soldiers . . . At this moment my curiosity was superseded by a sense of duty, and I began what I have since regarded as the best Sabbath day's work of my life. In the retreat during the night these men, who had been in the hands of the enemy for three days, were left behind. No relief had reached them at this early hour and I happened to be the first to come to their assistance. My first work was to carry them water, for the morning was very warm and they were all thirsty. On going to the pump I found two of them trying to fill their canteens. Both were wounded in the arm which they carried in a sling. One pumped and the other held the canteen using their sound limbs. As the time passed, other persons strolled in and rendered aid, but it was not until about noon that any part of the hospital corps arrived. And then only one surgeon and two assistants came to render their service. In the wagonshed a few boards were laid on some trustles and the work of amputation begun. I was asked to assist in holding the limbs of the subject operated on. The heat was intense and as the men had received no treatment for three days the odor from the wounds was repulsive. One after another was placed on the scaffold, put under the influence of chloroform and while the surgeon dextrously performed the operation, I would hold the limb until it was separated from the body. During all this time I suffered no nausea from the offensive smell or ghastly sight of bloody limbs that lay at my side. In due time the ambulances came and all of these wounded men were removed to the hospital in the town. While min-

gling among these men at the stone barn, I entered the
gangway between the stables and found my way to the
rear. A number were lying there in the dark . . . .[319]

The men of the Bucktail brigade were brave Pennsylvanians
who left their loved ones at home in defense of the Union. They
returned to Pennsylvania in the summer of 1863 to defend a ridge
none of them had ever heard of. Some escaped without a scratch
while others received grievous injuries. Those wounded that were
lucky died instantly while the less fortunate were left to die slowly
and painfully, their bodies riddled with large caliber bullets or torn
into many pieces by artillery shells. What were their last thoughts?
Some surely engaged in some form of prayer. Others may have
begged for someone to aid them in their suffering. Perhaps a few
sought some way to quicken the inevitable. For those who died in
the area of the McPherson barn its grand and imposing silhouette
was the last thing they ever saw. At least 100 Bucktails were killed
on the farm itself and another 60 died in the following days and
weeks. Initially interred on the battlefield near where they fell, their
bodies would eventually be sent home or re-interred at the Soldiers
National Cemetery in Gettysburg. We will never know their last
thoughts nor the sorrow felt by their families and friends upon the
news of their deaths but we can be sure that they gave their lives for
a most noble cause.

---

319. Leonard Marsden Gardner, "The Carnage at Gettysburg: As Seen by a Minister," *Civil War Times*, Vol. 3, No. 4
(July 1961), 14.

CASUALTIES OF STONE'S BRIGADE[320]
143rd REGIMENT PENNSYLVANIA VOLUNTEER INFANTRY
17 Killed, 21 Mortally Wounded (38 Total)

Name	Rank	Co.	Disposition
George W. Arnst	Pvt	K	Killed July 1
Henry C. Barnum	Pvt	H	Wounded July 1; died July 18 at a Baltimore hospital
William Benscoter	Pvt	F	Killed July 1
Charles W. Betzenberger	2nd Lt	I	Wounded in hand early in action; killed during retreat July 1
Charles Buckalew	Pvt	F	Killed July 1
George Chamberlain	Pvt	D	Wounded; died August 20 at a Philadelphia hospital
Wilson B. Connor	Pvt	C	Killed July 1
Westly Craigle	Pvt	D	Wounded; died in July at 3rd Div., First Corps Hospital
Benjamin H. Crippen	Color Sgt	E	Killed July 1
George W. Crocker	Pvt	H	Wounded in leg July 1; died August 24 at Fort Schuyler, New York
Thurston Dickinson	Pvt	E	Mortally wounded July 1
George Ogden Fell	Sgt	B	Mortally wounded in hip July 1; buried in German Reformed Church graveyard; removed to National Cemetery, plot E-51
Clackson Josiah Fry	Pvt	A	Killed July 1
Henry P. Hammersley	Pvt	K	Killed July 1
Jesse Harrison	1st Sgt	I	Wounded in right thigh July 1; died August 20 at Camp Letterman Hospital; daughter removed body next day
William M. Harvey	Pvt	F	Mortally wounded July 1
Adam C. Hazlet	Pvt	F	Killed July 1
David Hendershot	Pvt	E	Mortally wounded July 1
George W. Hoover	Pvt	D	Wounded; died August 16 of gangrene in a Philadelphia hospital
John E. Kink	Pvt	B	Mortally wounded July 1
Ernest Knierim	Cpl	E	Wounded in left lung July 1; died October 3 at the Pennsylvania General Hospital in York; buried grave #24 of hospital cemetery
George H. Mcginis	Cpl	C	Killed July 1
James L. Miles	Pvt	B	Wounded in leg July 2; died August 1 at a Baltimore hospital; buried in Louden Park Cemetery
Joseph Montonye	Pvt	D	Decapitated by artillery shell and killed July 3
Lyman R. Nicholson	1st Lt	G	Wounded in shoulder July 1; died July 13
John T. Nugent	Pvt	K	Killed July 1
John Pettenger	Pvt	A	Killed July 1
Calvin Slawbaugh	Pvt	A	Wounded July 1; died July 13 or 15; buried in wheat lot on High Street
Moses T. Smith	Pvt	C	Wounded July 1; died July 15 at a Baltimore hospital
Major Sorber	Pvt	D	Wounded in right thigh July 1; died August 12 at Camp Letterman Hospital; buried in hospital cemetery; removed to National Cemetery
Jacob Strouse	Pvt	C	Wounded July 1; died July 16; buried in east side of the Evergreen Cemetery
Daniel K. Thorn	Pvt	G	Mortally wounded July 1
Joseph Trip	Pvt	E	Killed July 1
Henry Ulrich	Cpl	B	Wounded July 1; died July 20; buried National Cemetery, plot B-57
William N. Williams	Cpl	K	Wounded July 3; died July 6; buried Jonathan Young's farm; removed to National Cemetery, plot E-13
Henderson Wolf	Pvt	I	Killed July 1
Jacob C. Yale	Pvt	I	Shot above left eye and killed July 1; may have been the first man in Stone's brigade to be killed at Gettysburg

320. John W. Busey, *These Honored Dead: The Union Casualties at Gettysburg* (Hightstown, 1996), 286-287, 291-295.

149th REGIMENT PENNSYLVANIA VOLUNTEER INFANTRY
52 Killed, 14 Mortally Wounded (66 Total)

Name	Rank	Co.	Disposition
Bernard Adams	Pvt	B	Killed July 1
Austin J. Ayres	Pvt	K	Killed July 1
Joseph H. Baldwin	Pvt	D	Killed July 1
William Bell	Pvt	F	Killed July 1
Paul Bickel	Cpl	H	Wounded July 1; died of gangrene August 2 at Satterlee Hospital, Philadelphia
James C. Blair	Pvt	I	Wounded July 1; died October 7
Henry G. Brehm	Color Sgt	C	Shot in the back July 1 while attempting to save the colors; died August 9 in a Philadelphia hospital
Charles Brewer	Pvt	G	Killed July 1
Thomas Callander	Pvt	F	Wounded in side and chest July 1; died July 23 at Third Division, First Corps Hospital
Albert O. Card	Pvt	K	Killed July 1
Andrew J. Caster	Pvt	C	Killed July 1
George F. Christian	Pvt	A	Killed July 1
William M Clarkswon	Pvt	I	Shot in head July 1; died July 19
John M. Cowden	5th Sgt	I	Wounded July 1; died July 20 at a York, Pennsylvania, hospital and buried there
Richard A. Curry	Pvt	B	Killed July 1
John Davis	Pvt	G	Killed July 1
David Dayton	Pvt	K	Killed July 1
Edwin W. Dimmick	Pvt	A	Killed by artillery shell July 1 and buried near McPherson barn
Ira G. Dodson	Pvt	F	Wounded in right femur July 1; died of gangrene September 20 at Letterman Hospital
Issac Z. Drake	Pvt	I	Killed July 1
Mathew Fetzer	Pvt	A	Killed July 1
William Fleming	Pvt	B	Killed July 1
James Forsyth	Pvt	H	Killed July 1
Robert Fox	Pvt	G	Wounded July 1; died July 16 at a Philadelphia hospital
Benjamin F. George	Pvt	B	Killed July 1
Curtis Gleason	Pvt	A	Killed July 1
Daniel F. Goss	Pvt	F	Killed July 1; buried in National Cemetery, plot B-10
John H. Hammel	Color Cpl	C	Shot in abdomen July 1; died September 25 in Baltimore
Daniel L. Hanould	Pvt	H	Wounded July 1; died July 10 at Third Division, First Corps Hospital
William H. Harmony	Pvt	I	Killed July 1 and buried on Michael Clarkson's farm
Ross Hood	Pvt	G	Killed July 1
Corwin Howe	Pvt	A	Killed July 1
Thomas B. Jones	Cpl	G	Wounded July 1; died July 25 at a Philadelphia hospital
David C. Kline	Pvt	H	Killed July 1; buried in National Cemetery, plot B-15
Mathew J. Laughlin	Pvt	I	Killed July 1
Henry Lentz	Pvt	C	Killed July 1
Ellis Lewis	Cpl	B	Killed July 1
Philip Lininger	Pvt	B	Killed July 1
James C. Logan	Cpl	G	Killed July 3; buried in National Cemetery, plot A-19
Issac Mall	Pvt	C	Killed July 1
Reuben B. Martin	Pvt	A	Killed July 1; buried next to Chambersburg Pike
Samuel T. McClure	Pvt	B	Killed July 1
Thomas J. McClure	Cpl	I	Killed July 1
Ashman C. McDaniels	Pvt	F	Killed July 1
John McDonald	Pvt	I	Killed July 1

Benjamin B. McPherson	Cpl	E	Killed July 1
Weston D. Millard	Pvt	F	Killed July 1; buried in Evergreen Cemetery
Jacob B. Nevil	Pvt	F	Killed July 1
Joshua Owen	Pvt	G	Missing in action July 1
Calvin Potter	Pvt	H	Killed July 1 and buried on Michael Clarkson's farm
Wison D. Race	Cpl	A	Shot in chest July 1; died July 24 at First Division, First Corps Hospital; body sent home by brother
Warren Raymond	1st Sgt	I	Killed July 1
Issac W. Rounds	Cpl	K	Killed July 1
William P. Sarge	Pvt	C	Killed July 1
Aaron W. Sattazahn	Pvt	C	Killed July 1
Alfred J. Sofield	Capt	A	Cut in two by artillery shell; buried in Evergreen Cemetery
Samuel Starr	Pvt	B	Killed July 1
Alexander M. Stewart	Sgt	D	Shot in lungs and spine July 1; died July 6 in a home in Gettysburg; buried in United Presbyterian Church; removed to Clinton, PA
Samuel R. Stilson	Cpl	K	Wounded July 1; died August 21 at a Philadelphia hospital
Reuben Stover	Pvt	H	Killed July 1
Henry Ulrich	Pvt	C	Killed July 1
William F. White	Pvt	F	Killed July 1
Nathan H. Wilcox	Cpl	A	Killed by artillery shell July 1 and buried near McPherson barn
Washington Wilson	Pvt	K	Killed July 1
Leroy S. Wodsworth	Sgt	F	Killed July 1
Clark Woodsworth	Pvt	F	Killed July 1

150th REGIMENT PENNSYLVANIA VOLUNTEER INFANTRY
31 Killed, 25 Mortally Wounded (56 Total)

Name	Rank	Co.	Disposition
Asher M. Beckwith	Pvt	G	Wounded; died July 21 at a Baltimore hospital
Fulton Bee	Pvt	G	Killed July 1
John Benson	Pvt	G	Killed July 1
John Boyer	Pvt	F	Wounded July 1; died; buried with an ambrotype in National Cemetery, plot D-74
Thomas Bryce	Pvt	A	Killed July 3
Henry Chancellor Jr	1st Lt	B	Shot in the left thigh July 1; leg amputated; died at the Seminary Hospital August 5
Charles Clyde	Pvt	I	Wounded July 1; died July 17 at Third Division, First Corps Hospital; buried in National Cemetery, plot B-58
John G. Coyle	Pvt	C	Killed July 1; buried in National Cemetery, plot E-44
Joseph F. Darborrow	Pvt	A	Killed July 3
Henry A. Fees	Pvt	D	Killed July 1
Zachariah T. Fink	Pvt	F	Wounded July 1; died
Alva H. Fish	Pvt	I	Wounded; died July 30; buried in National Cemetery, plot E-15
Hiram Fones	Pvt	I	Shot in the left hip July 1; died August 5 from a second hemorrhage
George W. Franklin	Pvt	I	Killed July 1
Frederick Fulk	Pvt	H	Killed July 1
Charles F. Gibson	Pvt	F	Wounded July 1; died
Frederick Gilmore	Pvt	C	Wounded July 1; died April 13, 1864, of wounds
Nathaniel P. Gowen	Pvt	C	Wounded in left leg July 1; leg amputated; died September 25 at Letterman Hospital; buried in hospital cemetery, plot D-64
Joseph J. Gutelius	Cpl	D	Killed July 1 and buried near the McPherson barn
Nathan Hand	Pvt	G	Killed July 1
William E. Henning	Cpl	D	Killed July 1

Lorenzo Hodges	Sgt	G	Wounded July 1; died July 14 at Third Division, First Corps Hospital
William J. Holmes	Cpl	G	Wounded July 1; died July 23 at Third Division, First Corps Hospital
Joseph Keen	2nd Lt	B	Killed July 1
Charles P. Keyser	Cpl	B	Killed July 1
Samuel Keyser	Pvt	A	Killed July 1
George Kimey	Pvt	C	Killed July 1
Alfred Lees	Cpl	A	Wounded July 3; died July 12; buried in National Cemetery, plot E-16
James P. Lukens	Pvt	E	Wounded July 1 and left on the field; died July 2; buried in Presbyterian Graveyard in Gettysburg, plot B-66
John May	Pvt	D	Killed July 1
Edward A. McFadden	Pvt	D	Killed July 1
Wesley Merrick	Pvt	G	Wounded and captured July 1; died July 20
Jonathan J. Miller	Pvt	F	Wounded July 1; died August 18
William R. Miller	Pvt	D	Killed July 1
Enos Mininger	Pvt	A	Wounded July 1; died July 20 at Third Division, First Corps Hospital
Harvey Morris	Pvt	A	Wounded in right leg July 1; leg amputated; died August 3 at Letterman Hospital
James Morris	Pvt	I	Suffered a skull fracture on July 1; died July 18 at a New York harbor hospital; buried in grave 657 of the Cypress Hill Cemetery
Jacob J. Mough	Pvt	I	Wounded July 1; died July 17 at Third Division, First Corps Hospital; buried in National Cemetery, plot B-59
Henry A. Mudge	Sgt	I	Killed July 1
Frank E. Northrup	Pvt	F	Killed July 1; buried in National Cemetery, plot A-14
Samuel Phifer	Color Sgt	I	Killed July 1
Issac Pilgrim	Pvt	G	Wounded in the hip and bowels July 1; died July 25 at Third Division, First Corps Hospital; buried in grave 5 of the hospital cemetery
Alonzo Platt	Pvt	C	Killed July 1
George Pollard	Cpl	A	Wounded July 1; died July 15 at Third Division, First Corps Hospital
Joseph Redman	Pvt	H	Killed July 1
Jesse Rex	Cpl	E	Killed July 1
Edward Rockhill	Cpl	E	Killed July 1
Joseph B. Ruhl	Cpl	D	Killed July 1; his sister found his grave on the field and took his body home
Hosea Smith	Pvt	C	Killed July 1
Samuel H. Spargo	Pvt	C	Wounded July 1; died July 14 at a Philadelphia hospital
William P. Swaney	Pvt	C	Killed July 1
Amos P. Sweet	Pvt	H	Wounded in right leg July 1; leg amputated; died July 15 in Peter Myers' house; buried in National Cemetery, plot C-37
John Swint	Pvt	A	Killed July 1
John W. Waddle	Pvt	F	Missing in action, July 1
Elias B. Weidensaul	Pvt	D	Killed July 1
George W. Young	Pvt	F	Wounded July 1; died July 8 or 9; buried in Associate Reformed Graveyard, plot B-37

Chapter 11

POST-BATTLE HISTORY OF THE McPHERSON FARM

"...pre-eminent and imposing..."

THE SENSE OF LOSS felt by the Slentzes upon their return must have been nothing short of profound. They and their farm had been victimized for five days. Apart from the actual battle damage to their house and barn they were confronted by buildings full of the dead and dying, bloody floors, tables, chairs, and the complete loss of their crops and belongings. An inventory of the damages revealed the loss of four horses, three cows and five calves, four hogs, forty chickens, and three turkeys. Their hay, four tons of it stored in the barn, had been used as bedding for the wounded or consumed by the innumerable horses encamped on the farm since July 1. Slentz's crops were destroyed by the trampling of the armies and expended ordinance and would never be harvested. Slentz claimed the loss of 18 acres of wheat, 16 acres of corn, 14 acres of oats and 18 acres of grass. Also lost was the family's garden that would have sustained them for the winter. Among their personal items either taken or destroyed were grain bags, a bushel measure, scythe, grain cradle, hay forks, cow chains, axe and mattock, shovel, halters, feed, bridles, collars, cord wood, flour, bacon, lard, and apple butter. From the house they lost silverware, quilts, comforters, shirts, sheets, towels, and candlesticks. The value of the Slentz's loss was assessed at $1080.69: $602.19 for personal property and $478.50 for crop loss.

It took nearly three months to make the farm inhabitable again.

During that time the Slentzes stayed at the Seminary. Sarah Slentz claimed that over 200 soldiers were cared for in their house and barn until they could be safely moved to other more appropriate medical facilities about the town. Two soldiers had been buried in their garden, one of them had been wrapped in a quilt from the house.

Edward McPherson was in Washington during the battle but returned the following week to view the field and check his property. Since he owned only the property, he had no right to claim damages to the crops or Slentz's personal possessions, but he could claim damage to the building and fences. He later said that he found the farm in a state of "great dilapidation" though the 1863 Brady photograph shows little evidence of this. There were undoubtedly numerous bullet and shell scars in the buildings and considerable damage to his fences. But considering the ferocity of the fight that took place here, both McPherson and Slentz must have been grateful that the buildings were still standing and in fairly good condition. Some of their neighbors to the south, the Bliss family for example, were not as fortunate.

Having lost nearly everything, it must have been a difficult winter for the Slentzes. But it appears that by 1867, the Slentzes had recovered much of what they had lost. The family continued to work the farm until 1895 when their house tragically burned down.

In 1868, Edward McPherson sold the farm to land speculators named Riley Hamilton and Jesse Emerson. They later sold the farm to the owners of the Springs Hotel who owned the property until 1904 when it was purchased by the United States government. Sadly, by that time the barn was the only structure still standing that was witness to the battle.

By April 6, 1895, the stone portion of the house had been replaced with a two-story frame section that allowed more room for the Slentz family. On that day, a faulty flue in the kitchen fireplace (located in the original Breadon log home) caused a fire that engulfed the entire structure and an adjacent shed. After the 1895 fire and the farm's abandonment, the buildings fell into disrepair and were eventually removed by the War Department in 1904 or 1905. Evidence of the buildings existence is still apparent today. There is a mound of earth and a pile of whitewashed bricks just southeast of the barn and in a small grove of trees where the original Breadon house once stood. The bricks may in fact be from the original kitchen fireplace.

When the National Park Commission received ownership of the McPherson Farm on Christmas Eve 1904, the McPherson barn became the only building owned by the park that was associated with the fighting on the First Day's battlefield. Winter precluded a thorough evaluation of the barn's condition or any restorative work. When the weather broke, Colonel John P. Nicholson rode out to the McPherson Farm for a careful examination of the historic structure. He was clearly displeased with his first inspection of the barn and described:

> The wall on south side is bulged out about six inches along center of wall; there is not a stable door on east side of barn, but one on the frame building attached to main barn on north side; the weather boarding on east side of barn is about one-half torn off and what boards are there are no good.[321]

The approach of summer meant the barn could finally receive some much needed repairs. The Commission's engineer, Colonel Emmor B. Cope, drew up specifications for the barn's "repair and restoration" and mailed them out to four bidders. Only one bid was eventually received, that of a John C. Irwin, who bid $460.50 on the contract. The Commission decided to accept the bid. Irwin was required to attest to his reliability in complying with the submitted specifications, and on June 1, 1905, wrote: "I will submit to specifications for repairing barn and tearing away sheds for $460.50."

In June the local newspaper reported that work on the McPherson barn was to begin, but inferred that the majority of the work was to be dedicated to the repair of the decaying woodwork. This, along with Irwin's statement that he was to tear away the sheds, seems to indicate that the deteriorating stone wall on the south end of the barn was not of great concern to Irwin. It may have been contracted out to someone else, or perhaps the Park did

---

321. John P. Nicholson, Journal, March 13, 1905, 15, GNMP.

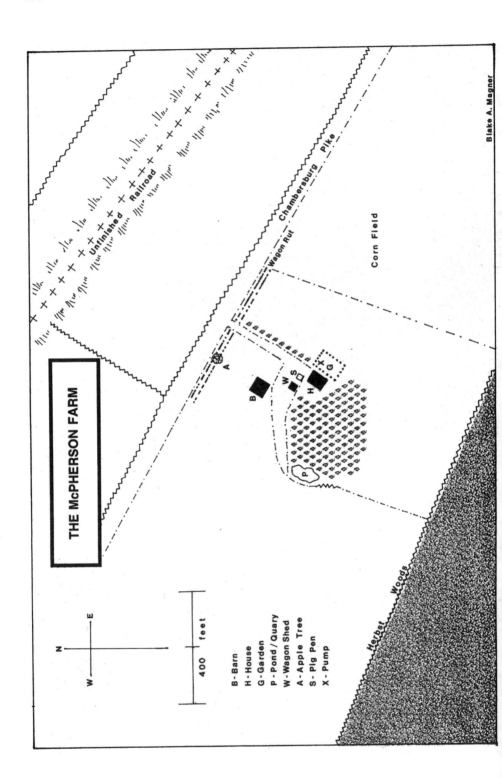

THE McPHERSON FARM

N · S · E · W

400 feet

B - Barn
H - House
G - Garden
P - Pond / Quary
W - Wagon Shed
A - Apple Tree
S - Pig Pen
X - Pump

Unfinished Railroad

Chambersburg Pike

Wagon Rut

Corn Field

Herbst Woods

Blake A. Magner

the repairs on the masonry themselves. But nothing in the Commission's records discusses anyone else but Irwin doing any work, carpentry or masonry.

The barn was supposed to be "preserved in its original state as far as possible," but it is clear from before-and-after photographs that this has not been the case. Apparently, what Irwin did was to tear down the broken down lean-to sheds on the barn's west side. It appears that these sheds were the same lean-tos that show in the 1863 Brady stereo view. Irwin also tore off the large north-end lean-to, which was added by Slentz sometime after the battle. Unfortunately, when he reconstructed the west-end lean-to bays, he shortened their previous length by about ten feet, thereby only approximating the earlier construction and not preserving the actual building appearance. From 1905 through 1977, the National Park Service continued to preserve the non-historical replacement by Irwin.

When Irwin repaired the cracked stone wall on the south end of the barn, he was already working with a wall that had been altered from its appearance at the time of the battle. The walls were originally stone from the foundation to the gable. By the late 1880s, however, the south gable was made of vertical siding and contained pigeon holes cut at intervals into the siding. It is possible that sometime after the battle the wall had collapsed or was threatening to collapse and Slentz or one of its owners had replaced the gable with the vertical siding. The evidence of a collapse was obvious in 1905, when Nicholson noted the center bulge and the cracking in the wall. In order to repair the crack and bulge, Irwin tore down and rebuilt only the center section of the stone wall to just about the eaves, where it met the 1880s vertical siding. He did not replace the embrasures that were present. In addition, after dismantling the frame wagon shed affixed to the north end of the barn, Irwin repointed the north gable wall, but did not replace the deteriorated plastered date stone cartouche. While the Gettysburg Park Commission was cost-effective in their approach to the barn's restoration, they were not particularly meticulous in regard to preserving the barn in its original state. Nearly everything Irwin replaced had become an adaptation: the shortened lean-to bays, the embrasureless south wall, and a north gable without its historic date stone cartouche. Additionally, by shortening the lean-to bays, he was forced to revise the roofline of the barn, even going so far as to change the location of the double-hung wagon doors.

Following its "restoration," the farm was rented out to a local farmer. Shortly thereafter the historic McPherson barn would require even more extensive repairs. It is unclear who exactly is to blame for this, possibly the Commission or perhaps the farmer himself. Regardless, on September 9, 1917, poor drainage around the barn caused the north wall to collapse. Earlier photos show the stone and mortar of the wall to be disintegrating. The mortar may have been hastened in its deterioration by the removal of the wagon shed that had protected it for twenty years. Presumably the combination of pulverized mortar and poor drainage may have caused a shifting of the foundation and walls, thus leading to its collapse.

Shortly after its collapse and an inspection by Nicholson and Cope, a contract for the reconstruction of the wall was given to Charles Kappes, a local stone hauler and mason who had been working with the Commission since the 1890s to lay foundations for monuments and was presumably well-known and reliable. Apparently some cursory work was done to stabilize the walls and roof until Kappes could start the work. Unfortunately, we are left once again without specifications, working drawings, or photographs of the preconstruction condition of the barn. In an effort to ameliorate the drainage issue, Kappes rebuilt the wall on a concrete foundation. The park laid 4-inch terracotta pipe to assure that the drainage problems on the sloping ridge would be reduced. In addition, about half of the east stable wall and about half of the west foundation wall were supplemented with concrete foundations which required that they be removed and rebuilt. Perhaps in an effort to reduce costs and presumably with the approval of the Commission, Kappes began to cut corners. While the east stable wall was replaced nearly as it had been (with the exception of the concrete foundation), the west foundation wall was rebuilt excluding the vented window which had originally been there. Unfortunately, the part of the wall that rose above the foundation level was never rebuilt at all. Perhaps it was felt that in light of its being obscured from view by the attached lean-to bay, it could be forsaken in order to save money.

To replicate the exterior of the south wall, the gable of the north end was likewise finished with vertical board siding, and the stone wall only reached to a point above the eaves. For aesthetic purposes the Commission had the new yellow pine boards painted the color of the stone so that the old stone wall and new wood gable blended together when viewed from a distance. Like the current south wall, Kappes decided not to replace the ventilator embrasures but did, in an effort to keep some semblance of the historic appearance, put in false embrasures that did not go the whole way through the wall (in other words, the ventilator embrasures did not ventilate). To stabilize the walls from further stress, tie rods were put in the barn. Included in this was the attaching of a 10-foot-long steel angle bar to the exterior of the south wall. Other work completed by the Commission included the removal of the old wood shingle roof, and replacing it with a galvanized sheet metal roof. For the first time, lightning arrestors were attached to the ridge of the roof as a precaution against a lightning-ignited fire. A hospital tablet made in 1905 for the barn, but not attached to the north wall until 1907, was finally replaced. In an effort to protect the barn from vandalism, a door lock was purchased securing the barn from access.

For almost 20 years the barn was left in this condition. Then in 1936, the National Park Service, which now operated Gettysburg National Military Park and its historic structures, repainted the siding. No one then employed by the Park Service was probably aware of the reason for the stone colored paint on the gables, so it was whitewashed like the rest of the barn. To give it more of an "historic appearance" the NPS removed the metal roof and replaced it with new wood shingles. No further effort was made to restore the barn to its true historic appearance.

By the time the "Historic Structures Report" was written for the McPherson barn in 1958-1959, the building was mistakenly accepted as virtually unaltered and original. The architectural section of this report goes as far as to state that "further architectural investigation of this structure is not required. As far as can be determined all structural members are original except roof rafters." This erroneous and irresponsible statement was obviously written without appropriate investigation into the background of the farm or its structures.

A NPS memorandum dated March 20, 1973, condemned the current use and maintenance of the McPherson barn and requested funds for repair of the profound damage which has already occurred:

Memorandum To: Team Captain, Historic Preservation Team
From: Exhibits Specialist (Restoration)
Subject: McPherson Barn, Gettysburg NMP

An inspection was made on March 8, 1973, with Tom Harrison, Chief, Resources Management, Gettysburg National Military Park. Little could be seen of the interior because the upper story of the barn was full of baled hay and the bottom was full of manure. From the time this structure was built c. 1840, agriculture practices have changed drastically. Consequently, the use of the barn has changed. If this barn is to be preserved, the current practices will have to be altered. The storage of baled hay to the apex of the roof will have to be stopped. The weight of baled hay is about three times that of loose hay. Therefore, the barn is being subjected to loads it was never intended for. The results of these loads are evident, particularly in the south end of the barn which has moved about 8 inches and the forebay overhang has moved 3 inches. The original summer beam had to be replaced two years ago.[322] The barn is spreading apart at the rafter line. If this indiscriminate use continues, the upper portion will suffer irreparable damage. The barn is used as a feed lot operation, allowing cattle to run all winter in the barnyard and lower portion of the barn. The manure has built to a depth of five feet. This situation is subjecting the wooden posts carrying the upper portion of the barn and door jambs, to unusual and extreme wetting conditions. This building was never intended for this type of operation. The barnyard has from 12 to 18 inches of mud and manure. I find this a very objectionable condition. A program should be insti-

---

322. Despite the author's best efforts, no documentation of the replacement of the summer beam could be found in the NPS files.

tuted to alleviate these conditions as quickly as possible. Funds for the repair of this damage should be made available as soon as possible.

[Signed] James S. Askins
cc: Supt, GNMP, T. Harrison, GNMP

In 1977, National Park Service ranger and historian, Kathy R. Georg, produced the first accurate historical study of the McPherson Farm. It was this research that discovered the glaring problems with the continuing preservation efforts at the farm and was critical of the National Park Service's methods of maintaining the property:

What has happened since the 1959 Historic Structures Report is that the National Park Service has continued to commit itself to preserving construction work of the War Department and subverting the true historic appearance of the McPherson Barn. The structure so inextricably interwoven into the history of the First Day's Battle has become a twentieth-century patchwork. It is no longer the McPherson Barn that is being preserved, but the John Irwin-Charles Kappes barn. The stately and impressive barn which was vividly remembered by those Union defenders no longer exists. Its vastness and uniqueness were bespoken by its massive stone walls (now dwarfed and emasculated by the falseness of the pine siding) and its long lean-to sheds and roof-line (also curtailed and diminished in visual impact). A preservation of the existing McPherson Barn cheats the historian and the visitor by projecting a deception of a historic barn (if not THE most historic of the remaining barns in the Park). If historic preservation is at all related to the historic integrity of a structure, then it must surely cry out for the efface-ment of the latter-day alterations by those contractors who interfered with this building's architectural life. Of all the historic buildings in the Park, the McPherson Barn stands pre-eminent and imposing on its ridge of the battlefield's First Day. As the sole survivor of the events that took place there on July 1, 1863 it would be fitting to pay it due tribute by restoring it to its 1863 appearance, instead of perpetuating the "mask" and "costume" it now wears.[323]

The impact of the study was clear. By August 22, 1978, the National Park Service had employed the architectural services of Abraham Levy of Philadelphia who issued Commission No. 7803, *Specifications for Repair and Restoration, McPherson Barn, Gettysburg National Military Park, Gettysburg, Pennsylvania*. These design specifications called for the complete and authentic restoration of the McPherson barn to its original 1863 form and appearance. Some modifications were specified to compensate for structural weaknesses and poor drainage that were not an original part of the early nineteenth-century McConaughy barn.

The most recent restoration of the McPherson barn following these specifications was completed in October 1979. Sadly, in this case, those from the Gettysburg National Military Park who were charged with the supervision of the work were almost inexcusably derelict in their documentation of the restoration. No known photographs, drawings, or formal completion report exists. Why the extensive overhaul of such an important feature of the battlefield was so poorly documented by the National Park Service is a mystery. It is ironic that there exists more information about the early history of the farm than there does the most modern re-engineering and restoration. Abraham Levy, architect for the project, along with Arthur Vorhees, the National Park Service employee responsible for oversight of the project, have vanished. The author has, through various means, attempted to locate or determine the fate of these individuals without success. Some speculate that Levy has died, the location of his documents pertaining to the farm gone with him. Information from those who knew Vorhees say he retired, though a national search for him has been unsuccessful. All that is left is a vague, handwritten, and undated Completion Report by Mr. Vorhees which does not address the completion of all aspects of Levy's specifications. A transcript of Mr. Vorhees report follows.

---

323. Kathleen Georg, *"Edward McPherson Farm: Historical Study."*

Some punctuation has been added by the author for the purpose of readability:

Completion Report

The McPherson Barn located on Route 30 1 mile west of Gettysburg Pa was completed on Oct 29[,] 1979[.] The Preservation Crew of Gettysburg National Military Park removed the lean to sheds and rebuilt them to the configuration of the July 1, 1863[.] [T]hen the north gable end above the square of the building which had been replaced by wood in the early 1900s was removed and rebuilt with stone to match the existing building[.] [T]he pointing on the exterior of this wall was cut out and the concrete at a level below the stable windows was removed and stone laid from the window sill level to 6 inches below grade[.] The stone face area of the forbay was removed by numbering each stone and a foundation poured under the wall and the wall replaced[.] [T]he south gable end wall was removed from the square down to the Hay mow floor and rebuilt putting the air vents back in using a Brady Photo dating the 9th or 10th of July 1863 to locate the openings[.] [A]ll corners were replaced with a story pole and numbering system[.] [T]he general stone in the body of the wall were replaced as near as possible to the location determined by the Brady Photo. [T]he original stone wall of the South West wall of the barn was only repaired where needed[.] [S]teel work was placed in the North and South ends of the barn to tie the structure. The false vents of the North wall were cut through to allow ventilation for hay storage[.] [A]ll of the stone work was pointed.

The forbay was reframed using the historic methods of construction and resided[.] [A]ll of the wood was painted two coats.

All of the barn doors were reworked the hinges and catches repaired and primed and painted.

Spouting was re-hung to car[r]y off the water until such time the drainage can be properly done.

> The hay mow floors were repaired with native oak. The hay mow was reinforced with steel I beams and four inch steel post on concrete bases[.]
>
> Arthur R. Vorhees
Exh Spe[324]

Left with just incomplete documents, the historian is forced to rely on comparisons of the specified work versus the actual modern appearance of the barn to determine the extent of the 1979 restoration. Despite the National Park Service's poor documentation of the barn's restoration, to their credit, it appears today much as it did in 1863, though few original components of the barn still exist. Fundamentally however, we still see the building much as those who fought in its vicinity did over 135 years ago. Standing beside it we can imagine the view that presented itself to the men of Stone's brigade on that broiling July 1. Its imposing form seems to provide comfort and safety and beckons one to the shelter of its massive stone walls. It is easy to imagine how Stone's troops would have been drawn to it in search of salvation from the nearing Rebel onslaught. Conversely, we can also imagine the dread the Rebels felt in assaulting what appeared to be such a well-fortified ridge. The National Park Service, once neglectful of the historic appearance of the building, has been redeemed from its original mistreatment by rebuilding and re-engineering the barn and its foundation to ensure that our grandchildren may someday stand in its shadow and recall the heroic sacrifices of the men who selflessly fought and died there in the summer of 1863.

---

324. Arthur R. Vorhees, *Completion Report*, pertaining to the restoration of the McPherson barn. GNMP. This is a handwritten, undated draft of the final completion report. No formal documents regarding the 1979 restoration exist.

EPILOGUE

For nearly five hours on July 1, 1863, the untested Bucktails of the Second Brigade occupied and effectively defended the "key-point of the First Day's battle."[325] Despite their lack of battle experience, drunken commanders, and attacks on both flanks, these Pennsylvanians managed to inflict galling casualties on the brigades of Daniel, Davis, Brockenbrough, and Scales, and delay the Rebel advance long enough for defensive positions to be established on Seminary Ridge and Cemetery Hill. That the brigade was able to withstand repeated attacks on their right was partly due to the existence of the Railroad Cut whose steep sides made breaching the barrier difficult. Had the Cut not existed, it is unlikely that the Bucktails could have held out as long as they did without support. Given the loss of 64 percent of the brigade's strength between 11:30 A.M. and 4:00 P.M., the scorching July heat, and their dwindling ammunition, it is impressive that they were able to hold on as long as they did. Perhaps they fought so stubbornly because they were on their home soil or maybe they felt that they still needed to earn the right to the Bucktail name. More than likely it was a combination of the two. Whatever the reason, the Bucktails filled a critical role in the First Day's fight, one that's been largely ignored until now.

The color incident of the 149th Pennsylvania is unique in the annals of Civil War history. The colors were a source of fierce regimental pride, typically used to identify, inspire, and rally the troops. That they were advanced to a position beyond the Chambersburg Pike to draw fire away from the regiment is puzzling. It was an unlikely maneuver, not found in any military textbook of the time.

---

325. Abner Doubleday, *Chancellorsville and Gettysburg*, 139-140.

It is doubtful that Dwight misinterpreted Stone's orders to advance the colors; so we must assume that the two had come to this decision together. Whether the decision was inspired by fear or whiskey is a matter of speculation, but it is peculiar that the 149th Pennsylvania was the only regiment given orders to do so. Surely the 143rd Pennsylvania's colors were visible from Oak Hill and the 150th Pennsylvania's from Oak Hill and Herr Ridge. Why were they not advanced to draw fire from the brigade? If the real reason was to deceive the enemy, would it not have been prudent to do so with all three sets of colors? Perhaps this was yet another example of Stone's preference to the regiment he had organized the previous fall. That he and Dwight never explained the movement other than to indicate that it was to deceive the Rebels may have meant that there was no other reason. We can therefore decide that while unconventional it was effective, though certainly not in keeping with mid-nineteenth century military tactics where honor on the battlefield dictated a great deal. Whatever the reason, we can be relatively certain that the ruse saved lives during Daniel's second advance on the Railroad Cut. Conversely, after it was discovered that the colors were advanced from the main line, they served no purpose whatsoever being in the advanced position beyond the pike. Recalling them to the 149th Pennsylvania's position along the pike may have assisted in keeping the command organized during their retreat, and most likely would have saved the colors from capture along with the life of Color Sergeant Henry Brehm.

On the evening of July 1, Robert E. Lee recognized the importance of the Cemetery Hill position to the defense of the town of Gettysburg. For the next two days it would be the object of his attacks. Had his *en echelon* attack been successful on July 2, the Bucktails, who had taken position the night before on the western slope of Cemetery Hill, would have been directly in the path of the Rebel onslaught. Because of poor coordination and communication, the attack sputtered out when it reached Mahone's brigade of Anderson's division. Later that evening, the Bucktails were advanced to a position along Cemetery Ridge from where they would take part in repulsing the most famous charge in American history the following day. Those who survived would never be the same.

For many surviving Bucktails, the battle of Gettysburg was the focal point of the rest of their lives. They spent much of their time discussing it, corresponding with other survivors North and South, and taking part in reunions to memorialize what they had done there. Given all the time they spent recalling the events of those three days, it seems odd that only Thomas Chamberlin of the 150th Pennsylvania chose to save his story for posterity in book form. Perhaps the internal conflict between the regiments and the confusion surrounding the movements of the First Day discouraged those literate enough to publish an account. For whatever reason, it is the author's hope that this narrative of the Bucktails's struggle at Gettysburg serves to give the casual and professional historian a stronger understanding of the importance of their stand on McPherson's Ridge and do justice to those who fought and died for its defense.

APPENDIX A

THE COURT-MARTIAL OF
BRIGADIER GENERAL THOMAS A. ROWLEY

"In my opinion he was drunk..."

Brigadier General Thomas A. Rowley, a 55-year-old, politically active cabinetmaker-turned-court clerk from Pittsburgh, was elevated to the command of Third Division when Doubleday was promoted to command of First Corps on June 30, 1863. Rowley received this promotion as a matter of seniority, not because any of his superiors had an overwhelming sense of confidence in his military acumen, a fact that was made clear on July 1, 1863. Robinson had handled his division exceptionally when struck by Rodes's Division, and Wadsworth had made his detractors take notice with his courageous and stubborn fight in Herbst Woods. In stark contrast, Rowley had exercised little, if any, control over his two brigades, Stone's and Biddle's. He appeared to have spent nearly all of his time on the field with Biddle's brigade, having neither ridden over to see to Stone's condition nor to issue him orders. Despite his presence, Biddle commanded his brigade almost entirely without the assistance of Rowley. The first recorded mention of Rowley's presence and conduct was upon First Division's retreat through Gettysburg where a number of officers and soldiers witnessed him reeling in the saddle, giving ridiculous commands, and claiming that he was in command of First Corps. He "had become positively insane" wrote Lieutenant Colonel Rufus R. Dawes of the 6th

Wisconsin. "He was raving and storming, and giving crazy orders" which only served to add to the panic of the retreating Federals.[326] Antics like that would certainly not go unnoticed. Provost Marshal Clayton E. Rogers observed that "General Rowley, in a great excitement, had lost his own 3d division, and was giving General Wadsworth's troops contradictory orders, calling them cowards, and whose conduct was so unbecoming a division commander and unfortunately stimulated with poor commissary."[327]

The clear-thinking Lieutenant Rogers, exercising exceptional judgement and courage, placed the intoxicated Rowley under arrest and called upon Dawes's exhausted men to execute the order. Dawes summed up the confusing and awkward moment well when he wrote:

> Cool, courageous and efficient men, at that supreme crisis in the history of our country, brought order out of chaos. In the midst of this, Clayton E. Rogers rode up and boldly placed General Rowley under arrest, and called on me for bayonets to enforce the order. This was perhaps the only instance in the war where a First Lieutenant forcibly arrested a Brigadier-General on the field of battle. I saw all that transpired; and during the half hour of confusion, Rogers, who was well mounted, by his cool, clear headed and quick-witted actions, did more than any other one man to get the troops in line of battle.[328]

Taken to the rear, Rowley was relieved of his command and assigned to administrative duties in Portland, Maine, until his court-martial at Culpeper, Virginia, on April 23, 1864. He was charged with drunkenness on duty on the battlefield, conduct prejudicial to good order and military discipline, conduct unbecoming an officer and a gentleman, and disobedience of orders. Ironically, Colonel Edmund L. Dana of the 143rd Pennsylvania served as counsel for the accused. Brigadier General Lysander Cutler testified that upon entering the town, "[He] (Rowley) inquired my name. I gave

---

326. Lance J. Herdegen, "The Lieutenant Who Arrested a General," 29.

327. Ibid, commissary refers to whiskey.

328. Ibid. It is difficult to imagine the kind of fortitude exhibited by Rogers when he decided to arrest a general at such a turbulent time of the battle. He clearly had no doubt in his mind that Rowley was drunk or that what he was doing was obviously the correct action.

it. He replied with some oath which I don't recollect, that 'he would attend to me another day,' that I was of no account. It was considerable of an effort for him to keep in his saddle . . . He was reeling in his saddle." The court asked Cutler if he felt that Rowley was intoxicated so much as to be unfit for duty to which Cutler replied, "I think so." Colonel W. W. Robinson of the 7th Wisconsin said, "At the time I saw him (Rowley) I thought he was drunk." First Lieutenant Thomas W. Miller of the 55th Ohio recalled that, "In my opinion he was drunk on that day, between 3 & 4 P.M." Even Doubleday said that "at the close of the battle on Cemetery Hill I thought him under the influence of liquor . . . ." In his defense, Major W. T. Humphrey, a surgeon on Rowley's staff, claimed that the reason the general had trouble staying in the saddle was a result of boils on the inside of his thighs.[329] It is interesting to note that Dawes and Rogers, the two men most involved with his arrest, were never called to testify. Those that did gave less damning testimony than perhaps Dawes and Rogers would have. While many men testified on Rowley's behalf, some of them never had any significant contact with him that day. Strangely, some of the supporting testimonies came from the men of Stone's brigade who had no contact with Rowley until the evening of July 1 back on Cemetery Hill, potentially giving Rowley enough time to sober up and thus skewing their impression of his state.

In the end, Rowley tried to explain away the accusations made by claiming that his horsemanship was a result of his medical affliction and not drunkenness. The charges stuck, however, with the exception of the last, disobedience of orders. He was sentenced to be dismissed from the service until Lincoln intervened on his behalf. Rowley resigned on December 29, 1864.[330] He died suddenly on May 14, 1892.[331]

329. *Court Martial of Brigadier General Thomas A. Rowley.* Edmund L. Dana Papers, Wyoming Historical and Geological Society.
330. Ibid.
331. Death Certificate of Thomas A. Rowley. Copy GNMP.

APPENDIX B

THE STORY OF JOHN L. BURNS

"God bless you, old man."

The boisterous, combative, and frequently incredible John Burns was 69 years old when his town was invaded by Jubal Early on June 26, 1863. Born in Burlington, New Jersey, on September 5, 1793, Burns had served for 18 months in the War of 1812.[332] He is said to have survived the savage fighting at Lundy's Lane though there is no known evidence to support this claim. In later years, as the story of John Burns spread (typically through his own variations on the subject) he would often have difficulty substantiating many of his claims. Today, because so many versions of the John Burns story exist, it is difficult for historians to separate fact from fiction.

The fierce patriotism he had developed in the War of 1812 had not diminished with the passage of 50 years. Early in the Civil War he enlisted in the Honorable Edward McPherson's newly formed three-month, Company K, First Pennsylvania Reserves. Arriving in West Chester, Pennsylvania, he was begrudgingly turned away by those who thought him too old to fight.

In the spring of 1862, he was elected to the position of town constable. Despite the fact that early in his life he had been "given to dissipation," he performed his duties diligently and was more recently know for being a disciple of temperance. Those who knew

---

332. Samuel P. Bates, *Martial Deeds of Pennsylvania* (Philadelphia, 1886), 988; Adams County Historical Society Newsletter, Volume 17, Number 6, June 1990. He was listed as a private in the 2nd Pennsylvania Volunteer Light Infantry.

him in his drinking days now said of him, "never was a man more earnest," and, he adheres to "strict and total abstinence." Unfortunately, his term was short lived, losing the position in April of 1863 to John Barrett and Henry C. Hoover thus forcing him to return to his previous occupation as a town cobbler.[333]

Probably thought to be too officious in demeanor, he was taken prisoner by Early on Friday, June 26, 1863, and held until the Rebels vacated the town on Sunday the 28th. Promptly upon his release, Burns claimed to have captured a Confederate chaplain who was performing messenger duties for Early and Ewell. Along with the chaplain, he was rumored to have apprehended a number of Rebel guerrillas still loitering in the area. This story, conceived by Burns, was never substantiated. One is left to speculate how Burns, who had recently lost his authority as a constable, would have had the authorization to arrest anybody. It is possible that given his experience and with Rebels in the area, he may have been given limited law enforcement powers. It is equally possible that in this rural mid-nineteenth century community, an attitude of "once a constable, always a constable" may have prevailed, thus affording him some limited local authority. This, of course, is speculation and, like the story itself, cannot be substantiated.

In the early morning action of July 1, Burns was instrumental in assisting General John Reynolds in his quest to find a quicker route to bring up his troops. Burns is said to have shown Reynolds the route across the fields between the Codori farm and the Seminary. Burns was apparently impressed with the short work the Federal troops made of the intervening fences. "The pioneers made the fences fly with their bright axes," he is quoted as saying.[334]

Later that morning, with the battle raging to the west, Burns apparently approached two wounded Federal soldiers on the outskirts of town. "Ah, my lads," Burns said. "Your guns are needed over yonder; but you are bleeding; and are too weak to carry them; give one of them to me." Stunned by the peculiar request, the soldiers initially said no. "What do you want to do with it?" said one of the men. "Shoot the damn rebels," replied Burns. One of the soldiers finally consented and allowed Burns the use of his rifle. Filling

333. William A. Frassanito, *Early Photography at Gettysburg* (Gettysburg, 1995), 85.
334. Samuel P. Bates, *Martial Deeds of Pennsylvania*, 988.

his pockets with cartridges, the aging old soldier started for McPherson's Ridge.[335]

Sergeant George Eustice, of Company F, 7th Wisconsin, recalled the approach of John Burns:

It must have been about noon when I saw a little old man coming up in the rear of Company F. In regard to his peculiarities of dress, I remember he wore a swallow-tailed coat with smooth brass buttons. He had a rifle on his shoulder. We boys began to poke fun of him as soon as he came amongst us, as we thought no civilian in his senses would show himself in such a place. Finding that he had really come to fight I wanted to put a cartridge-box on him to make him look like a soldier, telling him he could not fight without one. Slapping his pantaloons-pocket, he replied, "I can get my hands in here quicker than in a box. I'm not used to those new-fangled things." In answer to the question what possessed him to come out there at such a time, he replied that the rebels had either driven away or milked his cows, and that he was going to be even with them. About this time the enemy began to advance. Bullets were flying thicker and faster, and we hugged the ground about as close as we could. Burns got behind a tree and surprised us all by not taking a double-quick to the rear. He was as calm and collected as any veteran on the ground. We soon had orders to get up and move about a hundred yards to the right, when we were engaged in one of the most stubborn contests I ever experienced. Foot by foot we were driven back to a point near the seminary, where we made a stand, but were finally driven through the town to Cemetery Ridge. I never saw John Burns after our movement to the right, when we left him behind his tree, and only know that he was true blue and grit to the backbone, and fought until he was three times wounded.[336]

---

335. Ibid.
336. Henry J. Hunt, "The First Day at Gettysburg," in *Battles and Leaders of the Civil War,* edited by Robert U. Johnson and Clarence Buel, 3:276.

Versions of his approach to McPherson's Ridge vary, but its clear that he made first contact with the 150th Pennsylvania and not the 7th Wisconsin. As discussed earlier, Burns fought alongside the Bucktails and the Iron Brigade throughout the afternoon's struggle eventually being wounded on the retreat to Seminary Ridge. As the story goes, the aged soldier was eventually struck in the side by a ball and temporarily immobilized. Regaining himself, he again rose but was struck down once more, this time in the belt buckle, doubling him over and again rendering him momentarily useless. Once again he returned to the action only to be permanently halted by simultaneous balls in the arm and leg.[337] Thinking himself grievously wounded and not wanting to be shot as a spy (he was wearing civilian clothes), he threw his rifle away.[338] Then, lying immobilized on the ground due to the loss of blood, he managed to bury his remaining cartridges with a knife he carried in his pocket. Later, when the Rebels came up, he was passed over for dead. About 6:00 P.M. that evening, he was found by a Rebel detail that inquired as to how he came to be there. Thinking quickly, he concocted a story about his ill wife who was in need of care. Burns had left town seeking the assistance of a young lady on the next ridge over when he became caught between the lines and wounded. Though not convinced by the questionable story, the party also knew he would cause them no more harm in his current condition and passed him by. Later that night, a kind Confederate provided the old man with a blanket and some water.[339]

Early the next morning, Burns decided to attempt to find some care for his wounds. He had lost a great deal of blood and he had no movement or feeling in his wounded leg. Gradually, painfully, he was able to drag himself to a nearby log home on the southwest corner of the intersection of the Chambersburg Pike and Seminary Ridge.[340] There he may have been taken into the loft where he received some basic care. Later that day, with the issue still in ques-

---

337. Again it is pure speculation as to the number of wounds Burns received. One account had him wounded as many as seven times. The only wound that we can be sure of is the wound in his ankle as evidenced by post battle photographs.

338. Some versions have Burns leaving his home and fighting with his flintlock and powder horn while others indicate that he picked up a rifle from a wounded soldier. Photographs of Burns after the battle show him with a rifle clearly not of government issue. If he did in fact fight with his flintlock and then threw it away on the approach of the Rebels, one must wonder how it was retrieved after the fight.

339. Samuel P. Bates, *Martial Deeds of Pennsylvania*, 988. Variations of this story have him looking for his livestock.

340. Tim Smith uncovered this information during his work on Lee's headquarters and the Thompson house.

tion on the Federal left, Burns was taken by wagon back to his home (rented from Edward McPherson) by a neighbor identified as Anthony Sullivan.[341] Arriving, Burns found that his home was now a makeshift hospital. His neighbors, thinking him dead, were surprised at his arrival.

After the battle, General Doubleday, in his official report remarked:

> My thanks are especially due to a citizen of Gettysburg named John Burns, who, although over seventy years of age, shouldered his musket and offered his services to Colonel Wister, 150th Pennsylvania Volunteers. Colonel Wister advised him to fight in the woods, as there was more shelter there; but he preferred to join our line of skirmishers in the open fields. When the troops retired, he fought with the Iron Brigade. He was wounded in three places.[342]

John Burns would have one more famous encounter in November 1863 with the arrival of President Abraham Lincoln, as was reported in the *Sentinel*:

> That afternoon, following the dedicatory services, the president, having heard of the exploits of John Burns, requested that a committee wait on Mr. Burns and inform him that the president desired an interview with him. At length, Mr. Burns appeared. The meeting was extremely cordial. Lincoln's first words were— "God bless you, old man."[343]

Later that summer, as his fame continued to grow (mostly through his own efforts), Burns began a new vocation, accepting money in exchange for guide services around the Gettysburg battlefield. Later his notoriety got him a job as the doorman at the state's legislative halls. Though the stories of his participation in

---

341. Samuel P. Bates, *Martial Deeds of Pennsylvania*, 988. Adams County Historical Society Newsletter. Volume 17, Number 6, June 1990. It is also possible that a passing farmer by the name of Nienstadt took Burns home.
342. Ibid.
343. Adams County Historical Society Newsletter, Volume 17, Number 6, June 1990.

battle were largely exaggerated, he was frequently asked to attend numerous patriotic gatherings and speak on the topic.[344] On February 4, 1872, at the height of his self-inspired fame, John Burns died and took with him the truth of his actual involvement in the fight for McPherson's Ridge.

344. Ibid.

Appendix C

SUCCESSION OF BRIGADE COMMAND
JULY 1, 1863

Colonel Roy Stone

Roy Stone was born in Plattsburg, New York, to Ithiel and Sarah (Gurner) Stone. Educated at Union College, he later took up residence in Warren County, Pennsylvania. At the start of hostilities in 1861, Stone organized a body of men that would eventually be assigned to Colonel Kane's original Bucktail regiment. Kane was ultimately detached with four companies for special service leaving Stone in command of the remaining six.

Stone's men fought courageously on the Peninsula under George B. McClellan, frequently performing tenuous skirmish duty at the head of the command. Under Stone's leadership, the regiment soon developed a reputation for bravery and excellent marksmanship. Desiring a full brigade of such men, Governor Andrew Curtin recalled Stone to Pennsylvania for the purpose of organizing an entire brigade of Bucktails.

Having helped to do so, Stone found himself in command of the Bucktail brigade when he led it forward into position on the McPherson Farm. Soon after Daniel's Tarheels crested the ridge and bore down upon the Bucktails, Stone received a severe and painful wound in the right hip, instantly crippling him. Unable to walk, he was carried back to the McPherson buildings where he was abandoned upon the retirement of the brigade.

Following the withdrawal of Lee from Pennsylvania, Stone recuperated from his wound in a Union hospital. The next year, despite protests by his surgeon, Stone rejoined his command and fought in the Wilderness. During the advance on the Plank Road, Stone suffered a fall from his horse, which reopened his Gettysburg wound and ended his military career. For his services he was brevetted brigadier general and retired from the army.[345]

Colonel Langhorne Wister

Command of the brigade devolved upon Langhorne Wister after Stone fell following the initial assault of Daniel's Tarheels. Born of Quaker parents in Germantown, Pennsylvania, on September 20, 1834, Wister was 28 years old when he first commanded the brigade on July 1, 1863. Born to William and Sarah (Fisher) Wister, he had been educated at the Germantown Academy but left at the age of 18 to enter into the iron business.

Wister was devoid of military knowledge when he enlisted in the Federal army a week after Fort Sumter. Assigned to the newly formed Bucktails (42nd Pennsylvania), he was soon elected captain of his company, apparently because of his assistance in recruiting. Wister fought with distinction under Major Roy Stone during the Peninsula Campaign and returned home with him to assist in the organization of the new Bucktail Brigade.

The confidence that he inspired led him to the leadership of the 150th Regiment Pennsylvania Volunteer Infantry. It was while in command of this regiment on July 1, 1863, that he would, by virtue of his seniority, be elevated to brigade command when Stone was shot down north of the Chambersburg Pike. His brigade authority was short lived, however, when he too was horribly wounded in the face and jaw. Through the pain and hemorrhage he somehow managed to remain in control until the bleeding became too much for him to speak clearly. As a result of his heroism, Doubleday made mention of him in his official report with a recommendation that he be brevetted brigadier general.

In February of 1864, Wister resigned his command and resumed the business of manufacturing iron in Duncannon, Pennsylvania.[346]

---

345. Samuel P. Bates, *Martial Deeds of Pennsylvania*, Philadelphia, 1875.
346. Ibid.

Colonel Edmund L. Dana

Colonel Edmund Lovell Dana became the third and final commander of Second Brigade on July 1 around 3 P.M. after Langhorne Wister finally succumbed to the hemorrhage of his horrible jaw wound. Born in Wilkes Barre, Pennsylvania, on January 29, 1817, to Asa Stevens Dana and Ann (Pruner) Dana, he was descended from Anderson Dana, who was listed as an inhabitant of Pittstown in 1772. Well known in the Wyoming Valley, the Danas were known to be a highly honorable family having held political, legal, and scholarly positions since their arrival in America in 1640. As a toddler, Edmund L. Dana moved with his family from Wilkes Barre to Eaton where he and his brothers and sisters grew up tending the family farm. Having attended school during the winter, Dana was preparing for college at the Wilkes Barre Academy when he was accepted at Yale College in October of 1835. Dana graduated three years later with engineering credentials and was immediately engaged in the construction of the North Branch Canal, which he completed in 1839.

Upon completion of the canal, Dana gave up engineering and began studying law under the Honorable Luther Kidder. On April 6, 1841, upon the recommendation of the examination committee, Dana was admitted to the bar and began a long and distinguished career.

The following year, Dana married Sarah Peters, daughter of Ralph Peters, who bore him one son, Charles.

Not long after he became an attorney, Dana was given charge of a large law firm owned by the Honorable George W. Woodward, which served the counties of Luzerne and Wyoming. In 1846, while managing the firm, the Mexican War broke out and Dana enlisted in the Company I, First Regiment Pennsylvania Volunteers. His leadership abilities and experience were quickly realized and Dana was soon elected captain of the company.

Arriving in Mexico, his company was assigned to the siege of Vera Cruz. Later they were present at the surrender of the city and castle of San Juan D'Ulloa. Dana's troops accompanied General Winfield Scott into the Mexican interior in 1847 and were actively engaged. In 1848, Dana's command marched to Mexico City and remained there until peace in June. Following the war, he returned to Pittsburgh, was mustered out on July 20, 1848, and at once returned to the practice of law.

In 1851, Dana ran for Congress in the district composed of Luzerne, Wyoming, and Columbia counties and lost. Two years later, in 1853, he became a candidate for the state Senate but lost to Charles R. Buckalew.

At the outbreak of the Civil War, he was commissioned major general of the Ninth Division Pennsylvania Militia where he served until appointed by Governor Curtin to be commandant of a camp of organization and instruction called Camp Luzerne. A few months later, having observed his aptitude for fighting developed during the Mexican War, he was elected colonel of the newly organized 143rd Regiment Pennsylvania Volunteer Infantry.

Dana was the third and final commander of the Second Brigade on July 1, 1863, after Wister relinquished control. After the battle of Gettysburg, the remnants of the First Corps were consolidated into the Fifth Corps. Serving with the First Brigade, First Division, Fifth Corps, the 143rd Pennsylvania was in the Wilderness on May 5, 1864, when they encountered a large force of the enemy and many, including Dana, were taken prisoner. Ultimately arriving in Charleston sometime in June, Dana was subjected to the fire of Federal guns during the siege of the city. On August 3, he was exchanged and returned to his command in early September.

Following the hard fighting during the winter of 1864-1865, the 143rd Pennsylvania, now greatly reduced in numbers, was detached to special service at Hart Island where they were assigned duty guarding Rebel prisoners. Here they stayed until mustered out on June 12 and 13, 1865. Dana stayed on until the end of August performing court-martial duty. For his gallant service he was brevetted brigadier general and mustered out on August 23, 1865.

His distinguished military career shined bright in the fall of 1867 when he was elected Additional Law Judge of the Eleventh Judicial District of Pennsylvania where he presided the full ten-year term. Under considerable pressure from his peers and against his earlier wishes, he accepted a nomination to preside for a second term. Unfortunately, Dana along with the rest of his party fell to the newly formed Greenback-Labor party which swept Luzerne County.

In his later years, Dana enjoyed hunting and fishing and had a strong connection to St. Stephen's Episcopal Church in Wilkes Barre. He served on the Wilkes Barre city council and was the first president of the Wyoming Valley Historical and Geological Society.

Dana died in 1887 at the age of 70 and is buried in Hollenbeck Cemetery in Wilkes Barre, Pennsylvania.[347]

347. George B. Kulp, *Families of the Wyoming Valley*, 1: 31-41

BIBLIOGRAPHY

149th Infantry Regiment. *Minutes of the Reunion Meetings of the Surviving Members of Company D, 149th Pennsylvania Volunteers.* n.p., 1905.

150th Infantry Regiment. *Reunion at Gettysburg and Dedication of Monuments.* Ann Arbor, MI: University Microfilms, 1969. Reprint of 1889 edition.

"A Complete Loss." *Star and Sentinel.* Tuesday, April 9, 1895.

Adams County Historical Society Newsletter. Volume 17, Number 6, June 1990.

Andrist, Ralph K. *The American Heritage History of the Confident Years.* New York: American Heritage Publishing Co., 1973.

Annals of the War, Written by Leading Participants, North and South. Originally published in the Philadelphia *Weekly Times.* Dayton, Ohio: Morningside Press, 1988.

Annual Reports of the Gettysburg National Military Park Commission, Washington, D.C.: Government Printing Office, 1895-1920.

Approvals of Requests, 1895-1918. GNMP library.

Arrington, Benjamin, T. *The Medal of Honor at Gettysburg.* Gettysburg, Pennsylvania: Thomas Publications, 1996.

Ashurst, Richard L. *Address to the Survivors of the 150th Regiment, Pennsylvania Volunteers.* Read at Gettysburg, September 25, 1896, by Brevet Major Richard L. Ashurst. Philadelphia: Allen, Lane & Scott, 1897.

Ashurst, Richard L. *First Day's Battle at Gettysburg.* Philadelphia, 1913.

Ashmun, George. "Union Light Guards," *Magazine of History*, Vol. III, Number 4, April, 1906, pp. 248-254.

Clearfield Raftsman's *Journal,* Clearfield, Pennsylvania, GNMP.

Bandy, Ken and Florence Freeland. *The Gettysburg Papers.* 2 Vols. Dayton, Ohio: Morningside Press, 1978.

Bassler, John H. *Reminiscences of the First Day's Fight at Gettysburg.* An Address Delivered Before the Faculty and Students of Albright Collegiate Institute, June, 1895. Myerstown, PA: Press of Myerstown Enterprise, n.d.

_____. *The Color Episode of the One Hundred and Forty-Ninth Regiment,*

Pennsylvania Volunteers, in the First Day's Fight at Gettysburg. Papers and Addresses of the Lebanon County, PA Historical Society, 1907, pp. 77-110.

Bates, Samuel P. *History of the Pennsylvania Volunteers, 1861-1865.* 5 Volumes. Harrisburg, Pennsylvania: B. Singerly, 1869.

_____. *Martial Deeds of Pennsylvania.* Philadelphia: T.H. Davis & Company, 1873.

_____. *The Battle of Gettysburg.* Philadelphia: T.H. Davis & Company, 1873.

Beale, James. "The Statement of Time on July 1 at Gettysburg PA 1863." In *Gettysburg Sources,* Vol. 3: 38-72. Baltimore: Butternut & Blue, 1990.

Beecham, Robert K. *The Pivotal Battle of the Civil War.* Chicago: A.C. McClurg & Co., 1911.

Bennett, Timothy. "Three Bucktails: The Ottos of McKean County." *Military Images Magazine,* No. 16 January/February 1995, pp. 24-25.

Biddle, Chapman. *The First Day of the Battle of Gettysburg.* Philadelphia: J. B. Lippincott, 1880.

Bloom, Robert L. *A History of Adams County, Pennsylvania 1700-1990.* Gettysburg: Adams County Historical Society, 1992.

Bradsby, Henry C. *History of Luzerne County, Pa.* Chicago: B. Nelson, 1893.

Buehler, Fannie J. *Recollections of the Rebel Invasion and One Woman's Experience during the Battle of Gettysburg.* Gettysburg, Pennsylvania: Star and Sentinel Print, 1900.

Buell, Augustus C. *At Gettysburg.* Washington, D.C.: The National Tribune, March 30, 1893.

_____. *Gettysburg: Complete Analysis of the Official Records.* Washington, D.C.: The National Tribune, June 12, 1890.

Busey, John W. *These Honored Dead: The Union Casualties at Gettysburg.* Hightstown, NJ: Longstreet House, 1988.

_____. *The Last Full Measure: Burials in the Soldiers' National Cemetery at Gettysburg.* Hightstown, NJ: Longstreet House, 1988.

Busey, John and David Martin. *Regimental Strengths and Loses at Gettysburg.* Hightstown, NJ: Longstreet House, 1986.

Calef, John. "Gettysburg Notes: The Opening Gun." *Journal of the Military Service Institution of the United States,* Vol. 40 (1907): 40-58.

Callis, J. B. "John Burns of Gettysburg." Washington, D.C.: *The National Tribune,* November 10, 1898.

Chamberlin, Thomas. *History of the One Hundred and Fiftieth Regiment Pennsylvania Volunteers.* Baltimore: Butternut & Blue, 1986. Reprint of 1905 ed.

Clark, Walter, ed. *Histories of the Several Regiments and Battalions from North Carolina in the Great War, 1861-1865.* Wendell, NC: Broadfoot, 1982.

Coddington, Edwin B. *The Gettysburg Campaign: A Study in Command.* New York: Charles Scribner's Sons, 1968.

Court Martial of Brigadier General Thomas A. Rowley. Edmund L. Dana Papers. Wyoming Historical and Geological Society, Wilkes Barre, PA.

Cumberland Township Tax Records, 1799-1895. Adams County, PA, Historical Society.

Dana, Edmund L. *Diary of Edmund L. Dana.* Edmund L. Dana Papers. Wyoming Historical and Geological Society, Wilkes Barre, PA.

Dawes, Rufus R. *Service with the Sixth Wisconsin Volunteers.* Marietta, Ohio: E. R. Alderman and Sons, 1890.

Death Certificate of Thomas A. Rowley. Copy GNMP.

Deeds, Adams County Courthouse, Gettysburg, PA. Deed Books B, L, Z, and AA.

DeLacy, Patrick. "Capt. DeLacy Describes Gettysburg Battle." *The Scranton Truth,* 1913, Scranton, PA.

Doubleday, Abner. *Chancellorsville and Gettysburg.* New York: Charles Scribner's Sons, 1882.

Dustman, J. H. "John Burns, of Gettysburg." Washington, D.C.: *The National Tribune,* July 2, 1914.

Dyer, Frederick H. *A Compendium of the War of the Rebellion Compiled and Arranged from Official Records of the Federal and Confederate Armies.* Dayton, OH: Morningside, 1979.

"Edward McPherson, Clerk of the U.S. House of Representatives." *Star and Sentinel,* October 16, 1867.

Edward McPherson, Claims file (National Archives, photocopy and transcription in GNMP files).

Elmore, Thomas L. "A Meteorological and Astronomical Chronology of the Gettysburg Campaign." *Gettysburg Magazine,* July 1995, No. 13: 7-21.

Faust, Charles F. *Genealogy of the 149th Pennsylvania Volunteer Infantry, 2nd Bucktails, 1862-1865.* Shillington, PA: C.F. Faust, 1993.

Foster, Catherine. "The Story of the Battle: By A Citizen Whose Home Was Pierced By Shells," *Gettysburg Compiler,* June 29 & July 6, 1904.

Frassanito, William A. *Early Photography at Gettysburg.* Gettysburg, PA: Thomas Publications, 1995.

Fulton, Dr. James. "Gettysburg Reminiscences. A Surgeons Story." Washington, D.C.: *The National Tribune,* October 20, 1898.

Gallagher, Gary W. *The First Day at Gettysburg.* Kent, OH: Kent State University Press, 1992.

Gardner, Leonard Marsden, "The Carnage at Gettysburg—As Seen by a Minister," Civil War Times, Vol. III, No. 4 (July, 1961).

Georg, Kathleen, R. "Edward McPherson Farm: Historical Study," GNMP, October 14, 1977.

Gettysburg Borough Tax Records, 1857-1863. Adams County, PA, Historical Society.

Glatfelter, Charles. Extracts from the Road Docket and Quarter Sessions Docket, Lancaster and York Counties, Pennsylvania. Unpublished paper, Adams County, PA, Historical Society, 1974.

Glatfelter, Charles H. and Arthur Weaner. *The Manor of Maske: Its History and Individual Properties*. Biglerville, PA: Adams County, PA, Historical Society, 1992.

Glover, Edwin A. *Bucktailed Wildcats*. New York: Thomas Yoseloff, 1960.

Green, Wharton J. *Sketch of the Second North Carolina Battalion, CSA*. Suffolk, VA: Robert Hardy Publications, 1987.

Hampton, George F. "Brave Old John Burns." Washington, D.C.: *The National Tribune*, May 7, 1914.

Harris, Avery. *Avery Harris Journal*. Brake Collection, United States Army Military History Institute, Carlisle, PA.

_____. *Personal Reminiscences*. Brake Collection, United States Army Military History Institute, Carlisle, PA.

Hartwig, D. Scott. "Never Have I Seen Such a Charge," in *High Water Mark: The Army of Northern Virginia in the Gettysburg Campaign, Programs of the Seventh Annual Gettysburg Seminar*, 1999.

Hassler, Warren W. *Crisis at the Crossroads*. Montgomery, AL: University of Alabama Press, 1970.

Herdegen, Lance J. "The Lieutenant Who Arrested a General." *Gettysburg Magazine*, January, 1991, No 4: 25-32.

Historic Structures Report—Part 1: McPherson Barn, GNMP files, 1959 approval date.

Hitchcock, Chauncey. "John Burns at Gettysburg." Washington, D.C.: *The National Tribune*, April 2, 1914.

Hofmann, John W. *Remarks on the Battle of Gettysburg. Operations on the Right of the First Corps*. Philadelphia: A. W. Auner, 1880.

Huber A. H. "The First Corps at Gettysburg." Washington, D.C.: *The National Tribune*, September 30, 1909.

Hubler, Simon. "Just the Plain, Unvarnished Story of a Soldier in the Ranks." *New York Times Magazine*, June 29, 1913.

Huidekoper, Henry S. Oration by Henry S. Huidekoper at the Reunion of the Survivors of the 150th Regiment, Pennsylvania Volunteers at Gettysburg, Pennsylvania, August 13th, 1894. n.p., 1894, GNMP.

_____. "The 150th Pennsylvania of Colonel Roy Stone's brigade at Gettysburg." Washington, D.C.: *The National Tribune*, April 2, 1914.

_____. "A Short Story of the First Day's Fight at Gettysburg." In *Gettysburg Sources*. Baltimore: Butternut and Blue, 1986.

Hunt, Henry J. "The First Day at Gettysburg." In *Battles and Leaders of the Civil War*. Edited by Robert U. Johnson and Clarence Buel. 4 Vols. New York: Century Co., 1884-1887, Vol 3, 255-284.

Jacobs, Michael. *Notes on the Rebel Invasion of Maryland and Pennsylvania and the Battle of Gettysburg, July lst, 2nd, and 3rd, 1863*. Philadelphia: J. B. Lippincott & Co., 1864.

_____. "Later Rambles Over the Filed of Gettysburg," in *Administrative History, Gettysburg National Military Park and National Cemetery, Pennsylvania*, United States Department of the Interior, National Park Service, 1991.

"John Burns of Gettysburg." Washington, D.C.: *The National Tribune*, August 19, 1886.

John Slentz, Claims file. Pennsylvania Historical and Museum Commission, photocopy and transcription in GNMP files.

Jones, Francis B. *Chronicles of Francis B. Jones*. Copy GNMP.

Kensil, John C. "A Gettysburg Coincidence." Washington, D.C.: *The National Tribune*, n.d.

Kieffer, Harry, M. "Recollections of a Drummer Boy." Washington, D.C.: *The National Tribune*, December 31, 1881.

Krumweide, John F. "A July Afternoon on McPherson's Ridge." *Gettysburg Magazine*, Vol. 21: 21-44.

Kulp, George B. *Families of the Wyoming Valley. Biographical, Genealogical, and Historical Sketches of the Bench and Bar of Luzerne County, Pennsylvania*. 2 Vols., Wilkes-Barre, Pennsylvania: E. B. Yordy Printer, 1885.

Ladd, David L. and Audrey J Ladd. *The Bachelder Papers: Gettysburg in Their Own Words*. 3 Vols. Dayton, Ohio: Morningside Press, 1994.

Leon, Louis. *Diary of a Tar Heel Confederate Soldier*. Charlotte, SC:: Stone Publishing Company, 1913.

Letter from Corporal Sanford N. Boyden, Company A, 149th PVI to Captain R. E. Gamble. March 15, 1906. Copy GNMP.

Malone, Dumas, ed. *Dictionary of American Biography*. 22 Vols. New York, 1946.

Marsch, A. T. "North Carolina Troops at Gettysburg." *Confederate Veteran*. No. 16: 516-517, 1908.

Martin, David. *Gettysburg July 1*, Conshohocken, PA: Combined Publishing, 1995.

Matthews, Richard. *The 149th Pennsylvania Volunteer Infantry Unit in the Civil War*. Jefferson, NC: McFarland, 1994.

_____. "The Jackson Guards: Company C, 149th Pennsylvania Infantry at Gettysburg." *Military Images Magazine*. No. 8: 16-25, (May/June 1987).

_____. "Bassler and His Jackson Guards." Lebanon County, PA, Historical Society, Vol. 17, No. 1, 1987.

McLean, James L. Jr. and Judy W. McLean. *Gettysburg Sources.* 3 Vols. Baltimore: Butternut and Blue, 1990.

McPherson, Edward. "Local History," *Star and Sentinel,* May 14, 1895.

Meade, George G. *Life and Letters of George G. Meade.* New York: Charles Scribners Sons, 1913.

Melchior, Sheads J., and Roger J. Dunn. Historian's Report: Old McPherson Farm House. GNMP files, n.d.

Meredith, Jaqueline M. "The First Day at Gettysburg." *Richmond Times,* April 12, 1896.

Metzger, Frank R. "The Honorable Edward McPherson, Citizen of Gettysburg," unpublished paper, Adams County, PA, Historical Society, 1933.

Miller, William J. *The Training of an Army. Camp Curtin and the North's Civil War.* Shippensburg: White Mane Publishing, 1990.

Nesbit, John W. "The Bucktails on July 1." Washington, D.C.: *The National Tribune,* February 26, 1914.

_____."Recollections of Pickett's Charge," Washington, D.C.: *The National Tribune,* November 16, 1916.

_____. *General History of Company D, One Hundred and Forty-ninth Pennsylvania Volunteers.* Oakdale, CA: Oakdale Printing and Publishing Company, 1908.

Nevins, Allen. *Diary of Battle: The Personal Journals of Colonel Charles S. Wainwright.* New York: Da Capo Press, 1962.

Nicholson, John P. Journal. Unpublished, GNMP library, 1893-1921.

Pennsylvania. Gettysburg Battlefield Commission. *Pennsylvania at Gettysburg. Ceremonies at the Dedication of the Monuments Erected by the Commonwealth of Pennsylvania to Mark the Positions of the Pennsylvania Commands Engaged in the Battle.* 2 Volumes. Edited by John P. Nicholson. Harrisburg: E. K. Meyers, State Printer, 1893; Harrisburg: W. S. Ray, State Printer, 1904.

Pfanz, Harry W. "The Regiment Saved, Colors Lost." *By Valor and Arms.* Vol. 3, No. 2, 1977.

Ployd, Naaman, K. "John Burns of Gettysburg." Washington, D.C.: *The National Tribune,* January 9, 1899.

Ramsey, William R. "The First Corps at Gettysburg." Washington, D.C.: *The National Tribune,* April 30, 1908.

Rauch, William H. *History of the Bucktails.* Dayton, OH: Morningside Press, 1988.

Robinson, John C. "The First Corps. Its Important Services at the Battle of Gettysburg." Washington, D.C.: *The National Tribune,* April 14, 1887.

Sauers, Richard A. *Advance the Colors!: Pennsylvania Civil War Battle Flags.* 2 Volumes. Harrisburg, PA: Capitol Preservation Committee, 1991.

_____. *The Gettysburg Campaign, June 3-August 1, 1863: Annotated Bibliography.* Westport, CT: Greenwood Press, 1982.

"Sergeant James Rutter: Gettysburg Hero." *Sunday Independent*, Wilkes Barre, PA May 28, 1989.

Shafer, John. "First in at Gettysburg." Washington, D.C.: *The National Tribune*, August 25, 1887.

Shue, Richard S. *Morning at Willoughby Run, July 1, 1863*. Gettysburg, PA: Thomas Publications 1995.

Smith, Timothy H. *The Story of Lee's Headquarters*. Gettysburg, PA: Thomas Publications, 1995.

Stewart, James B. "Battery B, Fourth United States Artillery at Gettysburg." *Sketches of War History*, Cincinnati, OH: Robert Clark & Co, 1896. Vol. 3: 180-193. MOLLUS.

Stiles, Robert. *Four Years Under Marse Robert*. New York: The Neale Publishing Company, 1903; reprint, Dayton, Ohio: Morningside, 1977.

Sword, Wiley. "Captain James Glenn's Sword and Pvt. J. Marshall Hill's Enfield in the Fight for the Lutheran Seminary." *Gettysburg Magazine*, January 1993, No. 8, pp. 9-14.

Tax Records, Cumberland Township, 1828-1832, Adams County, PA, Historical Society.

Taylor, Frank H. *Philadelphia in the Civil War*. Philadelphia: By the City, 1913.

"The Color Episode." Editorial, Washington, D.C.: *The National Tribune*, June 2, 1910.

"Two Dwellings Burned," *Gettysburg Compiler*, Tuesday, April 9, 1895.

U.S. Census for 1800, Pennsylvania, York County, Cumberland Township. National Archives microfilm, GNMP library.

U.S. Census for 1810-1850, Pennsylvania Adams County, Cumberland Township and Gettysburg Borough. National Archives microfilm, Adams County, PA, Historical Society.

U.S. Census for 1860, Pennsylvania, Adams County, Cumberland Township. GNMP library.

U.S. Direct Tax for 1798, Cumberland Township, York County, Pennsylvania. National Archives microfilm, GNMP library.

United States War Department, *The War of the Rebellion: A Compilation of the Official Records of the Union and Confederate Armies*. 70 Vols. in 128 parts, Washington, D.C.: Government Printing Office, 1880-1901.

Vautier, John D. "At Gettysburg: The Eighty-Eighth Pennsylvania Infantry in the Battle." *The Press*, November 10, 1886 in Gettysburg Newspaper Clippings, VI ("Relating to the Battle"), 124-126.

Vorhees, Arthur R. "Completion Report, pertaining to the restoration of the McPherson Barn," Gettysburg National Military Park.

Walker, J. A. "Some Stirring Incidents." *Philadelphia Times*, Saturday, March 17, 188? in Gettysburg Newspaper Clippings, VI ("Relating to the Battle").

Will Book F. Adams County Courthouse, Gettysburg, PA.

Winschel, Terrence J. "Heavy Was Their Loss: Joe Davis's Brigade at Gettysburg." *Gettysburg Magazine*, January, 1990, No. 2: pp. 5-14.

Zierdt, William H. *Narrative History of the 109th Field Artillery, Pennsylvania National Guard, 1775-1930.* Wilkes Barre, PA: Wyoming Historical & Geological Society, 1932.

INDEX

Archer, James J., 35
Ashurst, Richard L., 15, 17, 23, 93

Barlow, Francis C., 59
Bassler, John H., 61, 63, 65, 78, 82, 85
Baxter, Henry, 53, 57, 71
Beath, R.B., 123-124
Bell, Horatio, 16
Belle Plain, VA, 19
Biddle, Chapman, 25, 38, 73, 95, 151
Boyden, Sanford N., 38, 74, 77, 100
Brabble, E.C., 97
Breck, George, 47
Brehm, Henry G., 77, 78, 79, 81, 148
Brockenbrough, John M., 55, 68, 71, 74, 75, 86
Buell, Augustus C., 90
Buford, John, 32, 33, 34
Burns, John L., 44, 155-160

Calef, John H., 34, 35, 45, 47
Carpenter, John Q., 123
Carter, Thomas H., 44, 45, 47, 50
Chamberlin, Thomas, 44, 55, 63, 65, 67, 68, 73, 74, 103, 110, 149
Chancellor, Henry, 43
Chancellorsville, VA, 21
Clarkson, Michael C., 29, 30
Conner, Rodney, 63
Crippen, Benjamin, 85, 86
Crotzer, Henry W., 16
Curtin, Andrew G., 12, 161, 164

Cutler, Lysander, 34, 38, 47, 71, 75, 152, 153

Dana, Edmund L., 17-18, 37, 39, 47, 58, 65, 71, 73, 74, 84, 85, 86, 92, 93, 95, 96, 107, 109, 152, 163-165
Daniel, Junius, 53, 55, 57, 58, 59, 61, 63, 65, 68, 82, 95, 148
Davis, Joseph R., 35, 45, 71, 74, 75, 86
Dawes, Rufus R., 88, 93, 118, 151, 153
DeLacy, Patrick, 38, 68, 105, 111, 116
Doubleday, Abner, 25, 33, 34, 34, 35, 36, 37, 38, 47, 51, 59, 71, 73, 74, 113, 151, 159, 162
Dougal, William P., 37
Dwight, Walton, 23, 32, 44, 49, 50, 55, 57, 58, 59, 61, 63, 75, 77, 82, 83, 95, 148

Early, Jubal A., 32, 156
Emmitsburg, MD, 25
Ewell, Richard S., 47

Firearms
  Enfield rifle, 16, 18
Frederick, MD, 25
Fulton, James, 45, 102-103

Gamble, William, 47
Gates, Theodore, 39
Gettysburg Battlefield
  Baltimore Pike, 100, 101
  Bull Frog Road, 37
  Cemetery Hill, 36, 43,
    100, 101, 102, 103, 108, 109, 148
  Cemetery Ridge, 110, 111, 115, 148-149
  Chambersburg (Cash-town) Turnpike, 28, 32, 34, 39, 41, 45, 47, 49, 51, 62, 63, 65, 68, 74, 75, 78, 84, 87, 89, 90, 92, 93, 126, 147, 162
  Codori Farm, 37, 110, 156
  Copse of Trees, 113, 115
  East McPherson's Ridge, 47, 49
  Emmitsburg Road, 37, 110, 117
  Evergreen Cemetery, 85
  Fairfield Road, 38, 88
  Forney Farm, 55
  Gordon Road, 25
  Hagerstown Road, 28
  Herbst Woods, 36, 38, 39, 50, 119, 121-122
  Herr Ridge, 35, 36, 41, 47, 49, 50
  Leister House, 109
  Lutheran Theological Seminary, 36, 37, 38, 84, 92, 95, 128, 156
  McPherson Farm, 27-32, 39, 41, 45, 50, 67, 74, 78, 95, 119, 120, 121, 126-128, 130, 135-146, 161
  McPherson's Ridge, 35, 36, 39, 41, 44, 47, 49, 50, 53, 59, 71, 74, 84, 125, 149, 157, 158, 160
  Marsh Creek, 28
  Middle Creek Road, 25

Millerstown (Pumping Station) Road, 37
Mummasburg Road, 28
Oak Hill, 42, 44, 45, 47, 49, 50, 51, 71
Oak Ridge, 38, 51, 93
Peach Orchard, 37
Pennsylvania (later Gettysburg) College, 127
Railroad Cut, 36, 41, 55, 57, 58, 59, 61, 62, 63, 65, 71, 75, 78, 82, 84, 92, 95, 147, 148
Railroad Wood, 95
Sachs Covered Bridge, 37
Saint Xavier Catholic Church, 102
Schumacher House, 95
Samuel White Farm, 25, 37
Seminary Ridge, 28, 32, 38, 47, 75, 78, 87, 89, 92, 93, 95, 105, 107, 115
Taneytown Road, 107, 109, 118
Thompson House, 89, 90, 93, 96
Upper Marsh Creek Presbyterian Graveyard, 28
Willoughby Run, 28, 35, 38, 42, 43, 44, 55, 68
Wills Farm, 55
Gilmore, Samuel P., 63
Glenn, James, 95-96, 109
Gordon, John B., 125

Hall, James A., 35, 36
Harris, Avery, 23, 49, 59
Heth, Henry, 34, 35, 44, 68, 74
Hill, Ambrose P., 33, 68-69, 71, 85-86, 103
Hooker, Joseph, 21, 22, 25
Hopkins, George, 110
Hopkins, James A., 61
Howard, Oliver O., 36, 38, 59, 71, 74
Hubler, Simon, 34, 38, 43, 51, 62, 90, 100-101, 107-109, 111, 115, 116
Huidekoper, Henry S., 16, 17,

21-22, 33, 42, 63, 65, 75, 93

Irvin, John, 47
Iverson, Alfred, 51

Jacobs, Michael, 127
Johnson, Andrew, 31
Jones, Francis B., 42, 62, 65, 120, 124-125
Jones, George W., 41, 43, 49, 101-102, 109

Kane, Thomas L., 11, 12
Kensill, John C., 59
Kropp, John C., 84

Landregan, James, 12
Lee, Robert E., 32, 126, 148
Lehman, Franklin, 79, 80
Lewis, William G., 57
Lincoln, Abraham, 16, 17, 31, 153, 159

Marshall, James W., 102
McClellan, George B., 12
McCullough, Zarah, 41
McIntosh, David G., 45, 47, 59, 61
McKendrick, J.F., 121
McLean, William, 125-126
McNeil, Hugh, 12
McPherson, Edward, 27, 30, 31, 136, 155, 159
McPherson, John B., 30
McPherson, Robert, 30
Meade, George G., 25, 33
Meredith, Solomon, 34, 38, 50, 73, 95
Middleton, MD, 23
Miller, John T., 121
Morrow, Henry A., 125
Musser, John D., 42, 58, 62-63, 83, 84, 85, 89, 93, 96, 97, 103, 107, 111, 113, 115, 117, 118

Nesbit, John W., 96, 110, 115, 117
Noecker, Isaac B., 38, 62, 82

Paul, Gabriel R., 57, 71

Pegram, William J., 45, 47
Peiffer, Samuel, 63
Pender, William D., 86
Pennsylvania, towns, cities and features
Camp Curtin, 13, 15-16
Camp Luzerne, 18, 164
Germantown, 15
Gettysburg, 28, 29, 33, 96, 99-103, 126, 127
Harrisburg, 13, 15, 18
Kingston, 18
Philadelphia, 15
Phoenixville, 15
Smethport, 12
Perrin, Abner, 95
Perry, William L., 121
Pettigrew, J. Johnston, 32, 73
Phillips, Owen, 86
Pickett, George E., 116, 117, 118

Ramsey, William R., 67, 71, 92, 102, 107, 110
Rauch, William H., 12
Reichard, George N., 84, 85
Reynolds, Gilbert H., 45, 47
Reynolds, John F., 25, 33, 34, 36, 41, 73, 122, 156
Robinson, William W., 151, 153
Rodes, Robert E., 44, 51, 71
Rogers, Clayton E., 152, 153
Rowley, Thomas A., 25, 35, 38-39, 73, 99-100, 151-153
Russell, A.L., 16
Rutter, James, 84, 85, 101

Scales, Alfred M., 86, 95
Schurz, Carl, 36, 59
Slagle, Jacob F., 35, 93, 105
Slentz, John T., 32, 122, 135
Spayd, Henry, 78, 79
Steinwehr, Adolph von, 36, 59, 103
Stevens, Thaddeus, 31
Stewart, James B., 53, 55, 58
Stone, Roy, 11, 12, 14, 15, 17, 18, 22, 38, 39, 41, 42, 44, 47, 49, 51, 53, 55, 59, 59, 75, 121, 151, 161-162

Units, Confederate
Army of Northern
  Virginia, 22, 32
Third Corps, 33
Heth's Division, 44, 119
Pender's Division, 119
Rodes' Division, 44, 49,
  51, 119
Daniel's Brigade, 71
42nd Mississippi, 78, 81
2nd North Carolina
  Battalion, 53, 57, 62, 65
13th North Carolina, 95
32nd North Carolina, 57,
  63, 75
38th North Carolina, 88,
  90, 96
43rd North Carolina, 57,
  92
45th North Carolina, 53,
  61, 62, 65
53rd North Carolina, 57
55th Virginia, 78
Carter's Artillery (Rodes'
  Division), 42, 44
Garnett's Artillery
  (Heth's Division), 42
McIntosh's Battalion
  (Artillery Reserve), 41
Pegram's Battalion (Artillery Reserve), 41, 61
Letcher (Virginia)
  Artillery (Brander's),
  59, 61
2nd Rockbridge (Virginia)
  Artillery (Wallace's), 107
Units, Union
Army of the Potomac, 11,
  17, 21
First Corps, 21, 25, 35, 36,
  59, 71, 73, 74, 99, 103,
  119, 151
Third Corps, 25
Eleventh Corps, 25, 36,
  71, 75, 96, 99, 101, 103
Third Division, 25

First "Iron" Brigade, First
  Division, 34, 35, 38, 73,
  83, 93, 118, 125, 159
First Brigade, Third
  Division (Biddle's), 25,
  38, 39
Second "Bucktail" Brigade,
  Third Division (Stone's),
  12-13, 17, 19, 21, 22, 23,
  25, 26, 36, 37, 38, 39, 43,
  45, 47, 58, 68-69, 73, 74,
  93, 96, 99, 105, 107, 115,
  118, 119, 130, 147, 148,
  149, 161, 162, 163, 164
24th Michigan, 125
147th New York, 35
55th Ohio, 108, 109
11th Pennsylvania, 90
42nd Pennsylvania
  Volunteers, 11, 12, 15,
  162
88th Pennsylvania, 123
114th Pennsylvania
  (Collis' Zouaves), 15
121st Pennsylvania
  Volunteers, 25
143rd Pennsylvania
  Volunteers, 17-19, 23,
  34, 36, 39, 41, 42, 43,
  45, 49, 51, 58, 59, 62,
  63, 65, 68, 83-84, 85, 89,
  93, 97, 100, 101, 103,
  107, 111, 113, 116, 117,
  119, 131, 148, 164
149th Pennsylvania
  Volunteers, 13-14, 15,
  17, 18, 22, 38, 41, 42,
  44, 47, 49, 50, 51, 55,
  58, 59, 61, 63, 67, 74,
  75, 77, 82, 83, 85, 86,
  93, 95, 100, 105, 109,
  110, 113, 115, 117, 119,
  120, 132-133, 147-148
150th Pennsylvania
  Volunteers, 15-17, 18,
  21, 23, 33, 37, 39, 43 41,

42, 44, 49, 50, 55, 59,
  63, 65, 67, 68, 71, 73,
  74, 75, 83, 86, 89, 92-93,
  101, 102, 103, 107, 109,
  110, 113, 119, 120, 123,
  133-134, 148, 149, 158,
  159, 162
151st Pennsylvania
  Volunteers, 39
6th Wisconsin, 36, 88, 90,
  93, 100
7th Wisconsin, 157, 158
First Corps Artillery, 45,
  92
Battery A, 2nd U.S.
  Artillery (Calef's), 34,
  45
Battery B, 4th U.S.
  Artillery (Stewart's),
  53, 87, 88, 90-91, 92
2nd Maine Battery, 34, 35
5th Maine Battery, 92
Battery B, 1st New York
  Light Artillery, 113
Battery L, 1st New York
  Light Artillery, 45, 50,
  92
Battery B, 1st Pennsyl-
  vania Light, 92
Battery C, 1st West
  Virginia Light Artillery,
  107

Wadsworth, James S., 33,
  36, 50, 53, 151
Wainwright, Charles S., 35-
  36, 39, 45, 50, 87, 99
Walker, J.A., 121-123
Washington, DC, 14, 16, 18
Wister, Langhorne, 15, 17,
  41, 44, 59, 63, 65, 75, 159,
  162, 163, 164
Wright, Ambrose R., 109-
  110
Wright, William H., 55, 105